ALL THAT MIGHTY HEART

UNIVERSITY OF VIRGINIA PRESS

Charlottesville & London

ALL THAT MIGHTY H·E·A·R·T

LONDON P·O·E·M·S

EDITED BY Lisa Russ Spaar

UNIVERSITY OF VIRGINIA PRESS

© 2008 by the Rector and Visitors of the University
of Virginia
Printed in the United States of America on acid-free paper

First published 2008

9 8 7 6 5 4 3 2 1

Library of Congress Cataloging-in-Publication Data
All that mighty heart : London poems / edited by Lisa
Russ Spaar.

    p.   cm.
  Includes index.
  ISBN 978-0-8139-2717-6 (alk. paper)
  1. London (England)—Poetry. 2. English poetry—
19th century. 3. English poetry—20th century. I. Spaar,
Lisa Russ.
  PR1195.L6A79 2008
  821.008'032421—dc22

2007045622

Contents

FOUR *Air* ⬡⬡⬡⬡⬡⬡⬡⬡

Acknowledgments

My first and deepest thanks must go to my friends and colleagues Stephen Cushman and Michael Levenson, who invited me to teach a course on the poetry of London in the University of Virginia Culture of London program at Regents College, where the idea for this anthology first glimmered. I'm grateful to my students in the London program, as well as to my stateside students, for their intelligence, enthusiasms, and ideas about the project.

I must also thank the tireless poet/curator Stephen Margulies, whose vision and prodigiously wide-ranging reading habits contributed invaluably to this book.

I appreciate the assistance of my other colleagues at the University of Virginia, especially Gordon Braden, Clare Kinney, and Jahan Ramazani, who offered keen, lively, and original insights into the poems gathered here. The staff of the Department of English, especially Cheryll Lewis, Barbara Moriarty, Lois Payne, and June Webb, and the personnel of the University of Virginia Library have offered gracious expertise and assistance. This project would not have been possible without support in the form of student research assistants from the Department of English, and a generous "small grant" award and additional support from Dean Karen Ryan and the Dean's Office of the College of Arts & Sciences at the University of Virginia.

Justin Quarry and Sarah Bishop helped to gather information for poems and permissions licenses in the initial stages of this project, and Joe Chapman and Julia Hansen offered invaluable, smart, and careful assistance in researching and crafting author biographies. Lytton Smith, Steven Barclay, and Howard Schwartz have been particularly helpful and supportive on this side of the pond, as Carrie Etter, Michael Horovitz, and especially Tony Rudolf have been on the other side.

I'm grateful to the staff at the University of Virginia Press, notably my editor, Cathie Brettschneider, and the assistant director and director of marketing, Mark Saunders.

Finally, I must thank my family for their long understanding in indulging my seemingly infinite obsession with "Infinite" London.

ALL THAT MIGHTY HEART

Introduction

London was a vital place within me long before I traveled there, emerging from the hot wind tunnels of the Russell Square tube stop in July of 1983. My heart beat wildly, and not just from the long climb up (the lift was broken). I was on fire that summer with the heady thrall of London calling—the Clash, Bloomsbury, the undertow of streets and squares mobbed by punks with stapled cheeks and faux arm casts, the seductive Thames and awakening South Bank, while, across green parks embellished with palaces, espaliered trees, and beds of roses, Lady Di and her young firstborn resided in the already intensifying pong of royal rumor. In truth, however, London, *my* London—a site of projection, imagination, myth, and historical, literary, familial ghosts—had been created over time and in no small part by poetry.

Like many non-Londoners, I knew the place first through verse. To me, growing up in a generic neighborhood of tract houses in suburban New Jersey, the very word "London"—which I had heard and recited in nursery rhymes long before I ever saw it written—opened within me a novel territory of golden lanes, a realm of kings and queens, of lopped and staked heads, rings of posies, treacheries, fires, oranges, lemons, the bells of St. Clement's. Perhaps most of all, "London" conjured an intriguing cosmos of bridges: bridges perpetually falling down and rebuilding themselves, bridges we'd mimic in kindergarten, joining hands to create a span that not only captured or released a playmate but bound us bodily to song and to place.

As I grew, London grew inside me. In childhood, I made happy excavations in the verses of A. A. Milne ("Whenever I walk in a London street / I am ever so careful to watch my feet"), Christina Rossetti ("Me you often meet / In London's crowded street"), and Stevie Smith ("The lion sits within his cage, / Weeping tears of ruby rage, / He licks his snout, the tears fall down / And water dusty London town"), as well as in the darker escapades of J. M. Barrie, Sir Arthur Conan Doyle, and Roald Dahl. Later, I found thrillingly suggestive inklings in the work of William Shakespeare, Charles Dickens, Elizabeth Barrett Browning, Iris Murdoch, Graham Greene, and many others. When I read about Geoffrey Chaucer's pilgrims in *The Canterbury Tales* setting off from the Tabard Inn in Southwark ("the finest victuals you could think, / The wine was strong and we were glad to drink"), I shared their excitement: could there be a more exhilarating place than London to begin an exploration of locale and self in verse?

Reading T. S. Eliot's *Four Quartets* in high school, I glimpsed into the heart of my own English heritage—reserved, stalwart, bound by routines and existential fears—in ways impossible to learn from living family members in whom those temperamental inclinations still thrived. My 11th-grade English teacher introduced me to Jonathan Swift's rollicking "A Description of a City Shower," its rhyming couplets reeking of eighteenth-century London street life: "Sweepings from Butchers Stalls, Dung, Guts, and Blood, / Drown'd Puppies, stinking Sprats, all drench'd in Mud, / Dead Cats and Turnip-Tops come tumbling down the Flood." Virginia Woolf's essay on going out to buy a pencil, "Street Haunting: A London Adventure," confirmed as meaningful my own propensity for wandering, for creative voyeurism, for the pleasures of watchful motion, of plundering the edges and the backs of things; through her, and Dickens, I learned to value the journey, the poetic process, the *walk,* as much as or more than destination, the *talk.* William Blake allowed me my rage at "mind-forg'd manacles" in all forms; Henry James effected a subtle, nuanced syntax of place that still mystifies and startles me. James Thomson's ur-urban, insomniac, Dantescan long poem *The City of Dreadful Night* conflated London for me with all cities, both real and imagined.

Perhaps it is the texture of possibility in cities that draws writers to them. Immense, complex, they are the largest of man-made entities. "The city is like poetry," wrote E. B. White in a famous essay about New York, "it compresses all life, all races and breeds, into a small island and adds music and the accompaniment of internal engines." London, ineffable crucible of humanity and nature, smoking with fashion, business, law, government, medicine, education, industry, commerce, literature, drama, art, music, politics, violence, religion, and technology, invites the overwhelmed wanderer of its literal and literary streets to respond. "I behold London," exclaims William Blake in *Jerusalem,* "a Human awful wonder of God!"

London occupies a fierce, undeniable position in literary imagination. Henry James was convinced of London's allure: "It is difficult to speak adequately or justly of London. It is not a pleasant place; it is not agreeable, or cheerful, or easy, or exempt from reproach. It is only magnificent. . . . It is the biggest aggregation of human life—the most complete compendium of the world. The human race is better represented there than anywhere else, and if you learn to know your London you learn a great many things." Beautiful and ugly, lyric and prosaic, parochial and cosmopolitan, progressive and backward, London has for centuries provided writers with a paradoxically intimate and protean text. "London has the effect," V. S. Pritchett has claimed, "of making one feel personally historic."

Seamus Heaney believes that one function of poetry is to write place into existence. Some of the poems in this anthology are by Londoners themselves, who find in poetry an inimitable way of articulating their native city. Other poets speak as strangers in a strange land: as foreigners or malcontents; eager, tentative, or aggrieved newcomers; deliberate outlanders. Many of the most striking poetic explorations of the city, in fact, come from outsiders whose alien eyes make of London a place as much imagined as reflected—sometimes idealized, often indicted. There is an Icelandic expression "Glöggt er gests augað," which literally translates as "clear/observant is the eye of a guest." In *The Place of Writing* (1989), Heaney—recalling the physical fact that the longer the lever, the less the force necessary "to move the mass and get the work going"—reminds us that geographical, temperamental, and cultural differences, whether small or immense, can provide a stance from which to move our subject matter with greater clarity. At times, he suggests, what is "intractable when wrestled with at close quarters becomes tractable when addressed from a distance." Any vision of place in poetry would seem to depend upon, to require, some vantage point or creation of apartness.

In his introduction to *A History of London* (1998), Stephen Inwood asserts that the story of London begins with foreigners: "To start with, London has always been a city that relied on migrants, from other parts of England, from Ireland or further afield, to maintain its economic, cultural, and demographic vigour. It was founded in an almost deserted spot by foreign conquerors, and its population has been replenished by invaders—with swords or suitcases—ever since." Peter Ackroyd, in *London: The Biography* (2000), concurs: "London has always been a city of immigrants. It was once known as 'the city of nations.'" John McLeod claims in *Postcolonial London: Rewriting the Metropolis* (2004) that "the presence in London of individuals and communities from overseas is as old as the city itself, and might be considered to constitute its definitive characteristic." He points out that an estimated three hundred distinct languages are spoken in London today. The various voices speaking across time, culture, and place in the poetry of London may help us to realize that this city has always been a place of transplantation, translation, and transformation.

With varying degrees of flexibility and xenophobia, the city has made room for its outsiders: dreamers, visionaries, expatriates, disaffected natives, tourists, and ghettoized immigrants. The London poems in this anthology span at least five centuries and represent many cultures and languages, including Judezmo, Punjabi, Russian, Spanish, French, Italian, Yiddish, Irish, Japanese, Chinese, Czech, and dialects and voices from the United States and Canada. Poetry, which *wants* to be of at least two minds, finds in London's stereoscopic, many-layered acoustics unique, provocative inspiration. What at least one commentator has called the "liminality of migrant experience" may be something all poets aesthetically seek and even contrive, recognizing in the resistances involved the vital processes of discovery.

Some voices, like those of Greek immigrant poet Rachael Castelete, speak from genuine, anguished marginality:

> If I had stayed in Salanik,
> Hitler would have killed me
> Just as he killed

All of my people.
Still, today in this city
I find myself
Miserable.

Whether created by locals or by poets who are not London-born, however, these poems approach London from an essential distance; they *mind* and *mine* the gap between self and place. Taken together, the poems juxtaposed here remind us that all of us, denizens, visitors, and transplants alike, are always, one way or another, exiled.

Each city has its own gestalt. One thinks of the *huzun* of Istanbul, the elegant frisson of Paris, Prague's secrecy, Dublin's density, the lofty, operatic bravado of New York, Madrid's *duende,* the *ostinato* decadence of Venice, the communal exoticism of Beijing. If there is a word for London's particular island fortitude—its brisk, labyrinthine spell—it may be found in Blake's evocation of the city as "Infinite," a scape both awful and awe inspiring. London, theater of nooks and crannies, possesses an unpredictable clamor, a rhythm of tidal, kinetic fluxes as intense in their reserve as in their public throng—a "weather" of surprises, of endurance. In *Writing London: The Trace of the Urban Text from Blake to Dickens* (1998), Julian Wolfreys speaks of London as not just *a* place but as "taking place," both as a text and in the texts it inspires. Its ineffability, he suggests, "may perhaps hold what we most desire: an anachronistic curiosity, a delight out of time, suggesting the eternal."

As many poetic visions of London exist as there are poets who have written about the city. Some sing her praises. "London, thou art of townes A per se. / Soveraign of cities, semeliest in sight, / Of high renoun, riches, and royaltie," wrote William Dunbar in the fifteenth century, proclaiming London "the flour of Cities all." Other poets fix on the chaos of the city, often connecting it with energies in the psyche. In Book VII of *The Prelude,* Wordsworth expresses his panicked excitement about the fate of the individual in London's "monstrous ant-hill on the plain / Of a too busy world!":

> Oh, blank confusion! true epitome
> Of what the mighty City is herself,
> To thousands upon thousands of her sons,
> Living amid the same perpetual whirl
> Of trivial objects, melted and reduced
> To one identity.

It has been noted, perhaps wrongly but with an element of poetic and historical truth, that London has its etymological roots in the Celtic word *londos,* meaning "fierce" or "wild," and in "Mourning and Melancholy," A. Alvarez acknowledges this primal, id-like pulse:

> Foxes are out on the Heath;
> They sniff the air like knives.
> A hawk turns slowly over Highgate, waiting.
> This is the hidden life of London. Wild.

Eliot's twentieth-century modernist elegy for Western civilization *The Waste Land* sets its stage of dispossessed humanity in London, the "Unreal city." Blake mythologized London while criticizing its political and social ills; in his poetic spectacle, London covered the whole earth: "In Felpham I heard and saw the Vision of Albion: / I write in South Molton Street, what I both see and hear / In regions of Humanity, in London's opening streets." Eiléan Ní Chuilleanáin, Paul Laurence Dunbar, Sylvia Plath, and Philip Larkin transform London into a stage for unsettling personal dramas or project onto its scrim of humanity private psychological and emotional losses, desires, and epiphanies.

Whether satirizing London or offering a litany of its delights—whether considering the city literally or figuratively—poets reacting to London are responding to energies at work and play not only in themselves but also in human civilization. I find it exhilarating to encounter in a London poem that is centuries old a fresh, contemporary shock of recognition, or in a London poem by a living poet an echo or specter of the ancient, abiding city. In her verse novel *The Emperor's Babe,* Bernardine Evaristo richly and anachronistically remixes mythical, ancient Londinium on a postmodern, streetwise turf. Welsh poet Dannie Abse peoples a Soho pub with Old Testament characters like Cain, Joseph, and Delilah:

> The Golden Calf closes. Who goes home? All
> tourists to Nod; psalmists from their pub crawl;
> they leave unshaved Soho to its dawn furnace
> of affliction, its wormwood and its gall.

Though this anthology wanders unchronologically, ahistorically, a brief survey of poetry in London may lend a context for the book's lively collage. In the Middle Ages and Renaissance, London was treated most often in prose pamphlets about London street life and in early seventeenth-century "city comedies" like *A Chaste Maid in Cheapside,* though there is also a fair amount of topographical, loco-descriptive verse, often in the tradition of Virgil's *Georgics,* and satire: in Swift, for example, we are treated to the redolent and discordant musics of overflowing sewers and ditches; in John Gay we learn how to walk the streets of the eighteenth-century city, with proffered advice ranging from proper footwear to when and how to keep or give "the wall" in order to avoid being baptized by the window-flung contents of a chamber pot. Shakespeare and other playwrights often set their scenes in London streets, pubs, and palaces in an act of metadrama.

Late eighteenth-century poets recognized incipient motions of disintegration and vision in London's mobbed streets and squares. With these poets, and the Romantics, came an evolving sense of interiority and of the role of a self in the world. In their musings, these early modern poets moved beyond topography and politics, tentatively approaching the city as a figurative body that questioned traditional notions of society, morality, and poetry. They brought to London their anxieties about the relationship of the individual to industrialization, urbanization, and change. In the twentieth century and afterward, poets, particularly those flooding into and out of the city from elsewhere, have attempted to cope with a sense of identity that is increasingly vexed, fluid, even fictive, in a globally connected city more and more resistant to individual sensibilities and ironically more vulnerable than ever to immediate, even apocalyptic terrors. Eliot's disaffected waste land seems almost innocuous when we consider other forces that now challenge human life in our time.

This anthology is organized around the primal elements—water, earth, fire, and air—in a way that I hope allows diverse poems to speak to one another. Some familiar and often-anthologized poems are here; others, often very beautiful and important ones, are not, though many of them may be found in the great number of fine anthologies of London poetry and prose that have already been published.

With so many riches to choose from, then, why another anthology of London poems? In the spirit of Clarissa Dalloway, I have felt inspired for some time to throw a big party, to bring together, at this particular juncture, at table, in the bar, on the dance floor, across sometimes vast temporal, cultural, and aesthetic terrains, poets and poems I admire, poetic responses to London that have, in part, created the city for me. This anthology, like any gathering, is eclectic and subjective, but I do think it brings into concert voices that have not yet often been heard together. The reader will also find here London poems and poets less well known but not less luminous, bridging time and space, talking back and ahead to poets dead, living, and yet to be born in a way that causes the collection itself, I hope, to beat—like London's island heart—with an energy enacting its arterial conduit of comings and goings, as well as providing, through its contrapuntal voicings, a vision of the city that may be larger, more "Infinite," than the sum of its parts.

WATER

We come from the sea. London, too, took its place, sometime in the late Neolithic period, on the banks and marshes of the river we now call the Thames. Forcefully tidal, the Thames connects London, essentially, with the ocean and the deepest, most unknowable sources of life, both local and beyond. As well as providing an avenue for approach, immigration, commerce, food, invasion, usurpation, violation, and departure, the Thames, whose name has pre-Celtic origins in "dark river," has long been a melancholic and ecstatic depository for everything from bodies and garbage to the dreamings and meditations of the pleasureborne, the enchanted, the desperate, the exiled, the alienated, and the power hungry. The poems in this section—which begins, as the book ends, with bridges—take in the full range of the Thames, from Ted Hughes's "filthy tonnage" to George Turberville's "stately stream." The force and glance of the river mirror the action of the poet: "I was

walking the Thames path east / as though I was water myself,"
writes Andrew Motion.

Robert Hayden's startling epistolary poem about the visit
of the ex-slave Phillis Wheatley to London in 1773 evokes the
many indentured and fugitive visitors brought by water to the
city. As Peter Ackroyd points out, "like the sea and the gallows,
London refuses nobody," and J. R. Ackerley, Stephen Cush-
man, and Max Hershman contemplate the river's haunting,
gravelike sorrows; Patience Agbabi, Fred D'Aguiar, and Carrie
Etter cast a London eye on the river's ambiguous development
over time. Bernardine Evaristo and Louis MacNeice imagine
Charon-like crossings, while Michael Donaghy and Anthony
Rudolf make of the self a bridge by which the reader finds it
"impossible / not to want to linger on this music" (Rudolf) or,
as Charles Wright says, not to "Step back and let your story,
like water, go where it will, / cut down your desires, / alone,
as you are, on the white heart of the earth."

EARTH

Spectacle of green squares, parks, and heath (the "lungs" of
London), streets, underground tunnels, crooked and crannied
eddies of roar, of silence, London stone is a temperamental,
volatile conglomerate of precincts: tower blocks, palaces, mar-
kets, ancient ruins, flourishing garden beds and window boxes,
temporary way stations of pub and museum, zoo and park and
taxi, and sanctuaries, both public and private. Dickens said he
needed streets to write, and many of the poets in this section
are peripatetic wanderers. Still others find inspiration in se-
questered garrets, flats, churches; even the homeless can find
temporary safety in their imaginations, as in Valery Larbaud's
"Trafalgar Square at Night":

Don't you feel, beggar girl, that it's lovely,
That it's truly delightful to be here
Wandering in this architectural desert
At the heart of the world's largest city, under the
    perpendicular
Stars, the malicious, blinking stars,
Hazy street lamps of the celestial city?

Andrew Salkey's "Notting Hill Carnival, 1975" throbs with the music that presides in street and soul:

Look at the frantic stamp-and-go,
the tugging muddle in the mind,
the heavy hesitation over play,
the forced glinting tone-and-flash.

Merle Collins floats the memory of a friend's island and New York City experiences over her transplanted life in London as the two women prepare to cross the street in Tottenham: "You see me laughing here? Is times have me chuckling so."

Poets like Eavan Boland and Amarjit Chandan remind us of the anguish of being removed from one culture to another. Kathleen Raine conjures a postlapsarian Eden in a city garden: "The very leaves of the acacia-tree are London; / London tap-water fills out the fuschia buds in the back garden, / Black-birds pull London worms out of the sour soil." Heaney's poem about the Underground reminds us that our graves are always beneath our feet:

And so by night and by day to be transported
Through galleried earth with them, the only relict
Of all that I belonged to, hurtled forward,
Reflecting in a window mirror-backed
By blasted weeping rock-walls.
                                        Flicker-lit.

FIRE

All cities are infernal. Their incendiary crowds, their potent centers of power and trade, their embolic politics make them susceptible to all sorts of conflagration and crises, individual and collective, from within and without. A subtext of blood and passion courses through London's red clay, ever ready to erupt in riot, flame, and violent pleasure, either literally, as in Linton Kwesi Johnson's "New Crass Massakah," or metaphorically, as when Blake's "hapless Soldier's sigh / Runs in blood down Palace walls." For centuries London has endured and risen again from a long series of ravaging fire, pestilence, and plague visitations which some writers, like Mary Adams, have seen as god-sent punishment and emblems of the city's damnation. The city has also been under fire in a barrage of terrorist attacks and wars. H. D. wrote in 1942 of the "Apocryphal fire" of bombs; Dame Edith Sitwell, who is said to have recited poems to refugees assembled in underground bomb shelters during the Second World War, described the falling fire as rain. Cocteau surreally transforms the fire of bombs into a conflation of rain, roses, and blood: "It must be red roses / . . . // Extraordinary roses / Where one can make out / The very mechanism of the nerves." Still other damaging fires rage within the individual. Larkin's moving "Deceptions" describes the rape of a young person. Charlotte Mew's "In Nunhead Cemetery" is a cry of anguished mourning: "I will burn you back, / I will burn you through." In "The Burning of Parliament, 1834," Steve Gehrke explores the connections between apocalypse and art—"Turner feels the fire / become a small glow that fills him as he paints, / like a secret growing in importance"—with a timeliness we cannot ignore.

AIR

London from the air: to the excited traveler or homecomer, nothing can be more alluring. Yet the air of London itself is a palpable presence with a forceful personality—leaden skies, once famously dense fogs, mizzle, blade-sharp winds, odors malodorous and fragrant, from pavement urine to the exquisite scarves of smoke that waft from Spitalfields curry stalls. This section of the book is full of the despair and reverie allowed by such extremes of weather and, as might be expected, also concerns vision, imagination, the "airy nothings" from which poets conspire to work their magic. Many of these poems speak directly to the connection between London skies and our desires, our mortality—the very stuff of poetry. In "By the Statue of King Charles at Charing Cross," Lionel Johnson asks, "Which are more full of fate: / The stars; or those sad eyes? / Which are more still and great: / Those brows; or the dark skies?" In a characteristically ironic poem, "Continuous Sky," Iain Sinclair writes: "can you believe 'The Poet' is now a wine bar in Mitre Street?" Ben Okri, on a pilgrimage to Primrose Hill, observes, "We saw the city and marvelled. / We dream the city better / Than it dreams itself." Lytton Smith, a Londoner now living in New York, writes in "Beyond London" that for him, all bridges are London bridges: "This is how London calls me back / to market-sound, to local stone." Finally, the wet skies of London return us to the river, the sea, and to the bridges where we begin our journeys, our crossing hearts, the heart of manifold London, as Davidson says, "beating warm."

What, then, is a London poem? As St. Augustine said of time, I know what it is until someone asks me. It is many things:

street poems, church poems, flat poems, park poems, pub poems, dub mantras, songs, dirges, laments, riffs, love poems, elegies, funny poems, political and social satires, nursery rhymes, parodies, and hymns of tribute, desire, despair, and more. Individually, but perhaps even more so collectively, these poems embody London in a way that reveals truths not only about urban identity and values but about ourselves in cities, about ourselves, about poetry.

Poets, restless watchers and wonderers, have responded over the course of London's history with enchantment and reservation to its dramatic cadences. In recent poems, if we sometimes feel a sense of entropy, anomie, or terror at what awaits us, we also experience the resiliency and complexity not only of the city over time but also of the human heart in an urban context.

Almost twenty-two years to the day after my first visit to London, I was there on July 7, 2005, on a family trip and was walking the streets when bombs began to go off beneath the ground and in buses across town. A kind of eerie silence fell over the city. Then the sirens began. Like others more directly and with greater cause to be affected by this violent assault on a beloved place, I was in that instant, and have been afterward, haunted by the forces of the city and of the individual that conspired in those crucial hours of aftermath: an augury of fear, threat, and of inevitable change, certainly, but also a responsive surge of tensile connectedness. In *The City in Literature: An Intellectual and Cultural History* (1998), Richard Lehan writes that "the city—for better or worse—is our future." Knowing London through poetry, we perhaps better understand ourselves—the nature of our civilization: our vulnerabilities, our multiplicity, our fickleness, our steadfastness, our wildness. In *The Confessions,* Augustine asks, "Who will hold the heart of man, so that it may stand still and see how steadfast eternity, neither future nor past, decrees times future and those past? Can my hand do this, or does the hand of my mouth by its little words effect so great a thing?" Poetry attempts to create this locus of stable eternity amid mutability. Wordsworth's "mighty heart" and Sitwell's "self-murdered heart," Johnson's "harrow af di fyah" and Davidson's "heart of London beating warm" remind us that London is not one reality, but many. The same might be said of our humanity.

WATER

Composed Upon Westminster Bridge, September 3, 1803

WILLIAM WORDSWORTH (1770–1850)

Earth has not anything to show more fair:
Dull would he be of soul who could pass by
A sight so touching in its majesty:
This City now doth, like a garment, wear
The beauty of the morning; silent, bare,
Ships, towers, domes, theatres, and temples lie
Open unto the fields, and to the sky;
All bright and glittering in the smokeless air.
Never did sun more beautifully steep
In his first splendour, valley, rock, or hill;
N'er saw I, never felt, a calm so deep!
The river glideth at his own sweet will:
Dear God! The very houses seem asleep;
And all that mighty heart is lying still!

Midriver

MICHAEL DONAGHY (1954–2004)

—and is a bridge: Now to either then:
child to lolly: spark across the wire:
lover to the target of desire:
Lambeth to Westminster: back again.
Verb's a vector not a monument,
but someone skipped a stone across this river
fixing its trajectory forever
in seven arches after the event
—so stops halfway and, neither there nor there,
but cold and rained on and intransitive,
watches London switch from *when* to *where,*
why to silence in the traffic jam,
thinks I can see the borough where I live
but here is temporarily who I am.

On Westminster Bridge

TED HUGHES (1930—1998)

A shattered army, Thames' filthy tonnage, tumbrils of carrion,
Not a beautiful spectacle
For the drinkers of history, or for me
Or my friends, this island's parallel issues.

Wordsworth's head went down here singing and the Isle Of
    Dogs ate it.
So now let us make our heads brass and proof,
O Thames
Plunder of your own defeat, O necessary sewer.

A woman somewhere upstream is washing the shirt of our
    future.
If you see her first she is powerless, full of blessings.
I have not seen her.
I see this disgorging of diseases, mud in a cupful,

And these refugees
Dragging the country down, without gesture or murmur, all
    heads bowed
In the lamentable press toward Atlantis
Under the bridges, with their attendant

Bladder dogs, their old corks and condoms . . .
The swan-voiced Elgar's decomposing—Let us all go down
    to exult
Under the haddock's thumb, rejoice

Through the warped mouth of the flounder, let us labour
    with God on the beaches!

Daily in the scarfing water
The banners
Fouled
And bandaging the shamed
Nameless battalions draining
Out of a dead lion—
                    deliquescing
To an officiation of blowflies.

Nightly this dark, feminine agony
Stemming from the womb no older than ever it was.

The Lover to the Thames of London, to Favour His Lady Passing Thereon

GEORGE TURBERVILLE (C. 1540–C. 1610)

Thou stately stream that with the swelling tide
'Gainst London walls incessantly dost beat,
Thou Thames, I say, where barge and boat doth ride,
And snow-white swans do fish for needful meat:

When so my love, of force or pleasure, shall
Flit on thy flood as custom is to do,
Seek not with dread her courage to appall,
But calm thy tide, and smoothly let it go,
As she may joy, arrived to siker shore,
To pass the pleasant stream she did before.

To welter up and surge in wrathful wise,
As did the flood where Helle drenchéd was,
Would but procure defame of thee to rise;
Wherefore let all such ruthless rigor pass.
So wish I that thou may'st with bending side
Have power for aye in wonted gulf to glide.

Impression du Matin

OSCAR WILDE (1854–1900)

The Thames nocturne of blue and gold
    Changed to a Harmony in grey:
    A barge with ochre-coloured hay
Dropt from the wharf: and chill and cold

The yellow fog came creeping down
    The bridges, till the houses' walls
    Seemed changed to shadows, and S. Paul's
Loomed like a bubble o'er the town.

Then suddenly arose the clang
    Of waking life; the streets were stirred
    With country waggons: and a bird
Flew to the glistening roofs and sang.

But one pale woman all alone,
    The daylight kissing her wan hair,
    Loitered beneath the gas lamps' flare,
With lips of flame and heart of stone.

Collecting the Ridges

CARRIE ETTER (1969–)

The skyline geometry and the April fog are again at odds. This prompts me, as usual, to go and stand on Hungerford Bridge to collect ridges of riverwater. Once the commuter exodus has passed, the god of the Thames—for it is too dark to lack a god—goes to his timpani and starts a tremor of sound. I stare harder to hear it. An hour into my work, a group of tourists asks me to take their picture a second time: in the first, they saw nothing they could name.

Valediction

ERIC PANKEY (1959–)

The Thames is a Mississippian umber beneath Blackfriars
　　Bridge,
The sky, an enclave of gray clouds.

Only the past is a deep-blue,
A glass prepared from silica and potash,
Oxide of cobalt pulverized as pigment.

The Marquis de Sade requested acorns be scattered over his
　　grave
So that an oak grove would obliterate its location.

If we let the dead bury the dead,
Perhaps all requests would be honored.
But the living bury the dead.

Small wonder the compass needle points its one way,
Shimmering like a divining rod's trance.
It was only today, I admit, that I noticed the anagram *Eros* in
　　the rose.

The Thames

MAX HERSHMAN (1891–?)

How many tears, my tears
Have you gulped down, Thames?
In the autumn evenings
Full of griefs and pangs?

When a choking grey fog
Spreads along your waves,
Along your waves, your shores,
And over us hangs.

When a choking grey fog
Spreads over your waves,
And the ships like spectres
In sad slumber lie.

And along the shores,
Across the misty wastes
A factory siren
Sends out a loud cry,

That strides like an echo
Through a dead desert,
And silently dies
In the misty height,

Where wrapped in darkness
A lonely lighthouse shines,

To guide the fishermen
On the sea at night.

How many tears, my tears,
Have you gulped down, Thames,
In those foggy evenings
Full of grief and moan?

Tell me, Thames, tell me, Thames—
And let the whole world know,
That on your free shores
Not always shines the sun.

Translated from the Yiddish by Joseph Leftwich

The Conjurer on Hammersmith Bridge

J. R. ACKERLEY (1896–1967)

He smiled at me in manner undismayed,
And then, with an expressive glance and shiver,
He flung his leg across the balustrade
    And dropped into the river.

Alone I watched his exit from the world;
Alone I ran to peer into the gloom,
And saw the way the swelling ripples curled
    Above his midnight tomb.

I watched his hat drift down upon the tide,
A witness of his scorn of God and men.
His head rose up as though dissatisfied,
    And slowly sank again.

Not mine the parting guest to speed or stay;
Not mine to interfere in private sorrow,
Or force a man who so disliked to-day
    To wait upon to-morrow.

I wondered would his last expiring breath
In other folk breed equal hate and strife.
I hoped he was enjoying more his death
    Than he had liked his life.

He rose no more. The waters ceased their stir;
But in my mind I saw him, pinched and sick,
Yet calm and smiling—like a conjurer
    About to do a trick,

A trick that was ineffable, sublime,
That loosed despair and hatred into space,
That flicked a human being out of time
      And never left a trace—

Except the hat. I watched it turn and sway
And wander from the place where he had drowned.
The conjurer had tricked himself away,
      And could not hand it round.

Between Blackfriars and Waterloo

STEPHEN CUSHMAN (1956–)

In a country that dreads most color
it looks so loud against the mud,

black mud and red blanket spread
by the edge of the shriveled Thames

as strollers crowd the Queen's Walk
to lean on a railing and study the scene:

two policewomen in black caps,
white shirts, neckties, two guys

in huge rubber boots dredging the shallows,
pewter clouds overhead that let the sun

leak on the mud through cracks of blue,
and under the blanket something uncovered

by outgoing tide, somebody's body
shrouded in my favorite color.

Shadwell Stair

WILFRED OWEN (1893–1918)

I am the ghost of Shadwell Stair.
    Along the wharves by the water-house,
    And through the dripping slaughter-house,
I am the shadow that walks there.

Yet I have flesh both firm and cool,
    And eyes tumultuous as the gems
    Of moons and lamps in the lapping Thames
When dusk sails wavering down the pool.

Shuddering the purple street-arc burns
    Where I watch always; from the banks
    Dolorously the shipping clanks,
And after me a strange tide turns.

I walk till the stars of London wane
    And dawn creeps up the Shadwell Stair.
    But when the crowing syrens blare
I with another ghost am lain.

Town in 1917

D. H. LAWRENCE (1885–1930)

London
Used to wear her lights splendidly,
Flinging her shawl-fringe over the River,
Tassels in abandon.

And up in the sky
A two-eyed clock, like an owl
Solemnly used to approve, chime, chiming
Approval, goggle-eyed fowl!

There are no gleams on the River,
No goggling clock;
No sound from St Stephen's;
No lamp-fringed frock.

Instead
Darkness, and skin-wrapped
Fleet, hurrying limbs,
Soft-footed dead.

London
Original, wolf-wrapped
In pelts of wolves, all her luminous
Garments gone.

London, with hair
Like a forest darkness, like a marsh

Of rushes, ere the Romans
Broke in her lair.

It is well
That London, lair of sudden
Male and female darknesses,
Has broken her spell.

A Letter from Phillis Wheatley

London, 1773

ROBERT HAYDEN (1913–1980)

Dear Obour
        Our crossing was without
event. I could not help, at times,
reflecting on that first—my Destined—
voyage long ago (I yet
have some remembrance of its Horrors)
and marvelling at God's Ways.

    Last evening, her Ladyship presented me
to her illustrious Friends.
I scarce could tell them anything
of Africa, though much of Boston
and my hope of Heaven. I read
my latest Elegies to them.
"O Sable Muse!" the Countess cried,
embracing me, when I had done.
I held back tears, as is my wont,
and there were tears in Dear
Nathaniel's eyes.

    At supper—I dined apart
like captive Royalty—
the Countess and her Guests promised
signatures affirming me
True Poetess, albeit once a slave.
Indeed, they were most kind, and spoke,
moreover, of presenting me
at Court (I thought of Pocahontas)—
an Honor, to be sure, but one,

I should, no doubt, as Patriot decline.
    My health is much improved;
I feel I may, if God so Wills,
entirely recover here.
Idyllic England! Alas, there is
no Eden without its Serpent. Under
the chiming Complaisance I hear him Hiss;
I see his flickering tongue
when foppish would-be Wits
murmur of the Yankee Pedlar
and his Cannibal Mockingbird.
    Sister, forgive th'intrusion of
my Sombreness—Nocturnal Mood
I would not share with any save
your trusted Self. Let me disperse,
in closing, such unseemly Gloom
by mention of an Incident
you may, as I, consider Droll:
Today, a little Chimney Sweep,
his face and hands with soot quite Black,
staring hard at me, politely asked:
"Does you, M'lady, sweep chimneys too?"
I was amused, but dear Nathaniel
(ever Solicitous) was not.
    I pray the Blessings of our Lord
and Saviour Jesus Christ be yours
Abundantly. In His Name,

                    Phillis

In a Perfect World

ANDREW MOTION (1952–)

I was walking the Thames path from Richmond
to Westminster, just because I was free
to do so, just for the pleasure of light

sluicing my head, just for the breeze like a hand
tap-tapping the small of my back,
just for the slow and steady dust

fanning on bricks, on cobbles, on squared-off
slab-stones—dust which was marking the time
it takes for a thing to be born, to die,

then to be born again. The puzzled brow
of Westminster filled the distance, ducking
and diving as long parades of tree-clouds

or skinny-ribbed office blocks worked their way
in between. The mouth of the Wandle stuck
its sick tongue out and went. The smoke-scarred walls

of a disused warehouse offered on close
inspection a locked-away world of mica
and flint and cement all hoarding the sun.

I was walking the Thames path east
as though I was water myself—each twist
and turn still bringing me out on the level,

leading me hither and thither but always
back to the hush of my clarified head,
into the chamber where one voice speaking

its mind could fathom what liberty means,
and catch the echo of others which ring
round the lip of the world. Catch and hold.

The buttery sun kept casting its light
on everything equally. The soft breeze
did as it always does, and ushered me on.

The London Eye

PATIENCE AGBABI (1965–)

Through my gold-tinted Gucci sunglasses,
The sightseers, Big Ben's quarter chime
Strikes the convoy of number 12 buses
That bleeds into the city's monochrome.

Through somebody's zoom lens, me shouting
To you, "Hello . . . on . . . bridge . . . 'minster!"
The aerial view postcard, the man writing
Squat words like black cabs in rush hour.

The South Bank buzzes with a rising treble.
You kiss my cheek, formal as a blind date.
We enter Cupid's Capsule, a thought bubble
Where I think, "Space age!," you think, "She was late."

Big Ben strikes six, my SKIN. Beat blinks, replies
18:02. We're moving anti-clockwise.

Greenwich Reach

FRED D'AGUIAR (1960–)

My mind fastened onto the rod.
The fishes that are there answer

my hook's singular enquiry
once they have read the correct line:

"How do I know for sure you're fish
and not pieces of old rubbish?"

Typically, fishes reply
by swallowing the hook and bait.

The Fisher of Men is Old Nick
who wields a big death-dealing stick,

he wishes to rejuvenate
the Thames, not with scaly fishes.

He means to relocate people.
The question his hook asks doubles

as his hungry hook's sole answer:
"You really don't want to die?

You don't really have to die!"
Death winks at you in the water.

Take the niggling, needling bait.
Let your poor soul swim off the hook

as a fish, not like those big fins
stuck at Woolwich, too proud to eat,

too fat to sink to a sound sleep.
A fish's nightmare: to be in air

like the thinner half of a line;
to belong to a school whose day

never ends, like those stranded fins
floating in a giant soup, the Thames.

FROM Omeros

DEREK WALCOTT (1930–)

He curled up on a bench underneath the Embankment wall.
He saw London gliding with the Thames around its neck
like a barge which an old brown horse draws up a canal

if its yoke is Time. From here he could see the dreck
under the scrolled skirts of statues, the grit in the stone lions'
eyes; he saw under everything an underlying grime

that itched in the balls of rearing bronze stallions,
how the stare of somnolent sphinxes closed in time
to the swaying bells of "cities all the floure"

petalling the spear-railed park where a couple suns
near the angled shade of All-Hallows by the Tower,
as the tinkling Thames drags by in its ankle-irons,

while the ginkgo's leaves flexed their fingers overhead.
He mutters its fluent alphabet, the peaked A of a spire,
the half-vowels of bridges, down to the crumpled Z

of his overcoat draping a bench in midsummer's fire.
He read the inverted names of boats in their element,
he saw the tugs chirring up a devalued empire

as the coins of their wake passed the Houses of Parliament.
But the shadows keep multiplying from the Outer
Provinces, their dialects light as the ginkgo's leaf, their

fingers plucking their saris as wind picks at water,
and the statues raising objections; he sees a wide river
with its landing of pier-stakes flooding Westminster's

flagstones, and traces the wake of dugouts in the frieze
of a bank's running cornice, and whenever the ginkgo stirs
the wash of far navies settles in the bargeman's eyes.

A statue swims upside down, one hand up in response
to a question raised in the House, and applause rises
from the clapping Thames, from benches in the leaves.

And the sunflower sets after all, retracting its irises
with the bargeman's own, then buds on black, iron trees
as a gliding fog hides the empires: London, Rome, Greece.

The Language of Love (III)
(FROM The Emperor's Babe)

BERNARDINE EVARISTO (1959–)

The sun is a gangrenous sore
oozing pus into the cesspit of the Thames;
when it has sunk
behind the mud flats of Southwark,
when I am indistinguishable from night,
I will swim to the ferryman,
sweet chariot of Charon,
coming for to carry me back
into oblivion,
to the waveless waters of my embryonic sac—
and as the waves make towards
the pebbled shore,
so will my minutes hasten towards my end,
leaving a crumpled pink frock,
and sling-backs.

Charon

LOUIS MACNEICE (1907—1963)

The conductor's hands were black with money:
Hold on to your ticket, he said, the inspector's
Mind is black with suspicion, and hold on to
That dissolving map. We moved through London,
We could see the pigeons through the glass but failed
To hear their rumours of wars, we could see
The lost dog barking but never knew
That his bark was as shrill as a cock crowing,
We just jogged on, at each request
Stop there was a crowd of aggressively vacant
Faces, we just jogged on, eternity
Gave itself airs in revolving lights
And then we came to the Thames and all
The bridges were down, the further shore
Was lost in fog, so we asked the conductor
What we should do. He said: Take the ferry
Faute de mieux. We flicked the flashlight
And there was the ferryman just as Virgil
And Dante had seen him. He looked at us coldly
And his eyes were dead and his hands on the oar
Were black with obols and varicose veins
Marbled his calves and he said to us coldly:
If you want to die you will have to pay for it.

Sea-Magic

WALTER DE LA MARE (1873–1956)

To R.I.

My heart faints in me for the distant sea.
    The roar of London is the roar of ire
    The lion utters in his old desire
For Libya out of dim captivity.

The long bright silver of Cheapside I see,
    Her gilded weathercocks on roof and spire
    Exulting eastward in the western fire;
All things recall one heart-sick memory:—

Ever the rustle of the advancing foam,
    The surges' desolate thunder, and the cry
    As of some lone babe in the whispering sky;
Ever I peer into the restless gloom
    To where a ship clad dim and loftily
Looms steadfast in the wonder of her home.

My Father's Flat

JAMES HARPUR (1956–)

Tugging apart the curtains every day
He always saw, three stories up, a grand
Sweep of the Thames, the trees of Battersea

And, squatting there, the Japanese pagoda—
Inflaming—a parody of a bandstand,
Its four sides flaunting a golden Buddha.

It glowed like a lantern near the glitzy braid
Of Albert Bridge at night.
                              If he had crossed
The river he might have heard *Renounce the world*

Escape the gilded lips or seen Gautama lying
In mortal sleep, his face relaxed, his flesh released;
Even in death, teaching the art of dying.

At night, across the river two golden eyes burn
Into the heavy velvet of the curtain.

Picture at an Exhibition

ANTHONY RUDOLF (1942–)

[*Old London Bridge* by Sir Samuel Scott
exhibited at Somerset House 1977]

The river is the mother of the city.
Over and over the bridge takes Londoners
to London from London, plays both ends
against the middle.
                    Half way through my life
in a house on that good bridge I am
a small boy, stand alone, and watch a small
boat move underneath my house, as late
cries from one bank mingle with new lights
from the other.
                    It is impossible
not to want to linger on this music.
Remembrance is colored in the making.

FROM *"A Journal of English Days"*

CHARLES WRIGHT (1935–)

—Chelsea Embankment, 5 p.m.: Whistler pastels squished
Down the fluted water, orange,
Tamarind, apricot
                    jade on the slate slip of the river,
Tug-ducks moored at the mudbanks,
Southbank light-string reflections stretched like struck and
    vibrating pipes,
The Thames rung softly
                        cross-river, and always a different note
Under the Albert Bridge, the Chelsea and out through town—
Or star-colored steps that sink
Beneath the sharkskin of the current
                                    down to the corridors
And bone-bossed gallery gates of the end.

—I keep coming back, like a tongue to a broken tooth,
Kensington Church Walk,
                        late afternoon,
Pigeons in bas-relief and frieze on the building's edge—
There is no sickness of spirit like homesickness
When what you are sick for
                            has never been seen or heard
In this world, or even remembered
                                except as a smear of
    bleached light
Opening, closing beyond any alphabet's
Recall to witness and isolate . . .

    .   .   .   .

A warm wind from the south and crows like mistletoe in
    the twist
And tuck of diluvial branches—

Stay out of the way and be conspicuous,
Step back and let your story, like water, go where it will,
Cut down your desires,
                alone, as you are, on the white heart of the earth.

EARTH

FROM *"The Burial of the Dead,"* The Waste Land

T. S. ELIOT (1888—1965)

    Unreal City,
Under the brown fog of a winter dawn,
A crowd flowed over London Bridge, so many,
I had not thought death had undone so many.
Sighs, short and infrequent, were exhaled,
And each man fixed his eyes before his feet.
Flowed up the hill and down King William Street,
To where Saint Mary Woolnoth kept the hours
With a dead sound on the final stroke of nine.
There I saw one I knew, and stopped him, crying "Stetson!
"You who were with me in the ships at Mylae!
"That corpse you planted last year in your garden,
"Has it begun to sprout? Will it bloom this year?
"Or has the sudden frost disturbed its bed?
"Oh keep the Dog far hence, that's friend to men,
"Or with his nails he'll dig it up again!
"You! hypocrite lecteur!—mon semblable,—mon frère!"

An Irish Childhood in England: 1951

EAVAN BOLAND (1944–)

The bickering of vowels on the buses,
the clicking thumbs and the big hips of
the navy-skirted ticket collectors with
their crooked seams brought it home to me:

Exile. Ration-book pudding.
Bowls of dripping and the fixed smile
of the school pianist playing "Iolanthe,"
"Land of Hope and Glory" and "John Peel."

I didn't know what to hold, to keep.
At night, filled with some malaise
of love for what I'd never known I had,
I fell asleep and let the moment pass.

The passing moment has become a night
of clipped shadows, freshly painted houses,
the garden eddying in dark and heat,
my children half-awake, half-asleep.

Airless, humid dark. Leaf-noise.
The stirrings of a garden before rain.
A hint of storm behind the risen moon.
We are what we have chosen. Did I choose to?—

in a strange city, in another country,
on nights in a north-facing bedroom,

waiting for the sleep that never did
restore me as I'd hoped to what I'd lost—

let the world I knew become the space
between the words that I had by heart
and all the other speech that always was
becoming the language of the country that

I came to in nineteen fifty-one:
barely-gelled, a freckled six-year-old,
overdressed and sick on the plane,
when all of England to an Irish child

was nothing more than what you'd lost and how:
was the teacher in the London convent who,
when I produced "I amn't" in the classroom
turned and said—"you're not in Ireland now."

When I Came to London

RACHAEL CASTELETE (1884?–1966)

When I came to London
I was a girl on a vacation.
I met this young man
And married him.

I had bad luck:
He left me in my old age.
And I, a fool,
Had never relished my youth.
I had brought him a good dowry,
Along with lots of Turkish liras.
I changed them into English money
And got nothing of it.

I came to this city
And have had to wage my own wars.
I thank my God
My children are all right.

If I had stayed in Salanik,
Hitler would have killed me
Just as he killed
All of my people.
Still, today in this city
I find myself
Miserable;
Today I find myself here,
And I cannot even buy a little bottle
of wine or raki.

Translated from the Judezmo by Stephen Levy

London Taxi Driver

DAVID DABYDEEN (1955–)

From Tooting, where I picked him up, to Waterloo,
He honked, swerved, swore,
Paused at the twin-tubbed buttocks of High Street Wives,
Jerked forward again,
Unwound the window as we sped along,
Hawked and spat.

The talk was mostly solitary,
Of the new single, of missing the pools by bleeding two,
Of some sweet bitch in some soap serial,
How he'd like to mount and stuff her lipsticked mouth,
His eyes suddenly dreamy with designs—
Nearly missing a light he slammed the car stop,
Snatched the hand-brake up.
Wheel throbbed in hand, engine giddy with anticipation.
As we toured the slums of Lambeth the meter ticked greedily.

He has come far and paid much for the journey
From some village in Berbice where mule carts laze
And stumble over broken paths,
Past the women with buckets on their heads puffed
With ghee and pregnancy,
Past the men slowly bent over earth, shovelling,
Past the clutch of mud huts jostling for the shade,
Their Hindu flags of folk defiant rituals
That provoked the Imperial swords of Christendom
Discoloured, hang their heads and rot
On bamboo pikes:

Now he knows more the drama of amber red and green,
Mutinies against double-yellow lines,
His aggression is horned like ancient clarions,
He grunts rebellion
In back seat discount sex
With the night's last whore.

Translating the English, 1989

CAROL ANN DUFFY (1955–)

. . . and much of the poetry, alas, is lost in translation . . .

Welcome to my country! We have here Edwina Currie
and the *Sun* newspaper. Much excitement.
Also the weather has been most improving
even in February. Daffodils. (Wordsworth. Up North.) If
    you like
Shakespeare or even Opera we have too the Black Market.
For two hundred quids we are talking *Les Miserables,*
nods being as good as winks. Don't eat the eggs.
Wheel-clamp. Dogs. Vagrants. A tour of our wonderful
capital city is not to be missed. The Fergie,
The Princess Di and the football hooligan, truly you will
like it here, Squire. Also we can be talking crack, smack
and Carling Black Label if we are so inclined. Don't
drink the H$_2$O. All very proud we now have
a green Prime Minister. What colour yours? Binbags.
You will be knowing of Charles Dickens and Terry Wogan
and Scotland. All this can be arranged for cash no questions.
Ireland not on. Fish and chips and the Official Secrets Act
second to none. Here we go. We are liking
a smashing good time like estate agents and *Neighbours,*
also *Brookside* for we are allowed four Channels.
How many you have? Last night of Proms. Andrew
Lloyd Webber. Jeffrey Archer. Plenty culture you will be
    agreeing.
Also history and buildings. The Houses of Lords. Docklands.
Many thrills and high interest rates for own good. Muggers.

Much lead in petrol. Filth. Rule Britannia and child abuse.
Electronic tagging, Boss, ten pints and plenty rape. Queen
   Mum.
Channel Tunnel. You get here fast no problem to my country
my country my country welcome welcome welcome.

The Double City

MONIZA ALVI (1954–)

I live in one city,
but then it becomes another.
The point where they mesh—
I call it mine.

Dacoits creep from caves
in the banks of the Indus.

One of them is displaced.
From Trafalgar Square
he dominates London, his face
masked by scarves and sunglasses.
He draws towards him all the conflict
of the metropolis—his speech
a barrage of grenades, rocket-launchers.

He marks time with his digital watch.
The pigeons get under his feet.

In the double city the beggar's cry
travels from one region to the next.

Under sapphire skies
or muscular clouds
there are fluid streets
and solid streets.
On some it is safe to walk.

The women of Southall
champion the release
of the battered Kiranjit
who killed her husband.
Lord Taylor, free her now!
Their saris billow in a storm of chants.

Schoolchildren of many nationalities
enact the Ramayana.
The princely Rama
fights with demons
while the monkey god
searches for Princess Sita.
I make discoveries and lose them
little by little.
My journey in the double city
starts beneath my feet.
You are here, says the arrow.

"The very leaves of the acacia-tree are London"

KATHLEEN RAINE (1908–2003)

The very leaves of the acacia-tree are London;
London tap-water fills out the fuschia buds in the back garden,
Blackbirds pull London worms out of the sour soil,
The woodlice, centipedes, eat London, the wasps even.
London air through stomata of myriad leaves
And million lungs of London breathes.
Chlorophyll and haemoglobin do what life can
To purify, to return this great explosion
To sanity of leaf and wing.
Gradual and gentle the growth of London Pride,
And sparrows are free of all the time in the world:
Less than a window-pane between.

A Description of London

JOHN BANCKS (1709–1751)

Houses, churches, mixed together,
Streets unpleasant in all weather;
Prisons, palaces contiguous,
Gates, a bridge, the Thames irriguous.

Gaudy things enough to tempt ye,
Showy outsides, insides empty;
Bubbles, trades, mechanic arts,
Coaches, wheelbarrows and carts.

Warrants, bailiffs, bills unpaid,
Lords of laundresses afraid;
Rogues that nightly rob and shoot men,
Hangmen, aldermen and footmen.

Lawyers, poets, priests, physicians,
Noble, simple, all conditions:
Worth beneath a threadbare cover,
Villainy bedaubed all over.

Women black, red, fair and grey,
Prudes and such as never pray,
Handsome, ugly, noisy, still,
Some that will not, some that will.

Many a beau without a shilling,
Many a widow not unwilling;
Many a bargain, if you strike it:
This is London! How d'ye like it?

Living in London (FROM *"Redcliffe Square"*)

ROBERT LOWELL (1917–1977)

I learn to live without ice and like the Queen;
we didn't like her buildings when they stood,
but soon Victoria's manly oak was quartered,
knickknacks dropped like spiders from the whatnot,
grandparents and their unmarried staffs decamped
for our own bobbed couples of the swimming twenties,
too giddy to destroy the homes they fled.
These houses, no two the same, tremble up six stories
to dissimilar Flemish pie-slice peaks,
shaped by constructor's pipes and scaffolding—
aboriginal like a jungle gym.
Last century's quantity brick has a sour redness
that time, I fear, does nothing to appease,
condemned by age, rebuilt by desolation.

The Garret

PAUL LAURENCE DUNBAR (1872–1906)

Within a London garret high,
Above the roofs and near the sky,
My ill-rewarding pen I ply
    To win me bread.
This little chamber, six by four,
Is castle, study, den, and more,—
Altho' no carpet decks the floor,
    Nor down, the bed.

My room is rather bleak and bare;
I only have one broken chair,
But then, there's plenty of fresh air,—
    Some light, beside.
What tho' I cannot ask my friends
To share with me my odds and ends,
A liberty my aerie lends,
    To most denied.

The bore who falters at the stair
No more shall be my curse and care,
And duns shall fail to find my lair
    With beastly bills.
When debts have grown and funds are short,
I find it rather pleasant sport
To live "above the common sort"
    With all their ills.

I write my rhymes and sing away,
And dawn may come or dusk or day:
Tho' fare be poor, my heart is gay,
    And full of glee.
Though chimney-pots be all my views;
'T is nearer for the winging Muse,
So I am sure she'll not refuse
    To visit me.

London Inside and Outside

AMY CLAMPITT (1920—1994)

Looked back on happily, the ivy-hung,
back-wall-embowered garden of our
pied-à-terre and domicile in Chelsea
seems oddly like some dream of living
halfway down the well that sheltered
Charles Dodgson's Elsie, Lacie
and Tillie—with those geraniums
in urns, that lily-of-the-valley
bed not quite in bloom, those churring
ringdoves, those thrushes murderously
foraging for earthworms: an exterior
so self-contained, a view so inward
that though at night we'd note
faint window-glimmerings eclipsed by ivy,
we seemed to have no neighbors either
to spy on or be spied on by.

Those strolls at dusk, the sidewalks
puddled underfoot, the streetlamps
an aloof processional (a footfall
once or twice, then silence)
at the hour not of the pulling down
of shades but rather of the drawing
in of curtains on their rods, with
an occasional small, to-be-savored
lapse—the glimpse in solitude
of the young woman meditatively
taking off her coat: or of

the table laid, the TV
in the dining room tuned to the news,
a South-Sea-bubble porthole open
on the mysteries of domicile,
of anchorage, of inside-outside!

The night we took the Underground
to Covent Garden, we found the foyer
at the opera a roofed-in waterfall
of crystal, the staircase we sat on
at the interval to eat our ices
carpet-luscious (even to the shod
sole) as a bed of crimson mosses,
the rose-red lampshades erotic
as hothouse hibiscus. Floated
overhead, a firmament of gilt
and turquoise; as that goes dim,
beneath the royal monogram the bell jar
of illusion lifts, and yet again
we're inside-outside: Norina's
rooftop vista (the duenna
furiously knitting) of a hot-bright
Bay of Naples. In the obscurity
of our neck-craning balcony, we
snuggled undetected. Outside there waited
a shivering, rain-speckled exodus among
dark gardens of the inevitable
umbrellas going up.

Strange Interlude

CAROL MUSKE-DUKES (1945–)

That hot summer in London
you were Ned Darrell. In South Ken,
we kept a bright flat, rented a paddle-

boat on the Serpentine, where you &
The Badger sat, moving. Galaxies spun,
swans drifted on their reflections. Up

from rehearsal, you kept on being him.
That far from you, I saw, was fiction.
At night, late, I'd lose myself in new chapters.

There—you stand at the mirror: Ned Darrell, worrying
his tie, gazing into my eyes through your reflection.
Murmuring about Nina in O'Neill underscript—what

the character thinks. Tugging at the silk knot,
frowning . . . *Isn't built to face reality, no writer is*
outside of his books. Then: *Got to help her snap*

out of this. I look out of the window, it's time
for you to go. *Help her snap out of this,*
I say, then laugh. But you look cross—

it's late, the car's outside. And see?
My own characters peer out of the mirror—
the one you and he left trembling.

FROM *"Roman de la Rose"*

NISHIWAKI JUNZABURŌ (1894–1982)

It was ten years ago at noon when I parted from John.
In October I was to go to university, and John
went to hell.
The two of us ran through foggy London,
got scolded for climbing up on the roof of the British
    Museum.
Later John's picture appeared in a literary magazine.
Surrounded by pencils, he jutted out his cheekbones with a
    grand air.
When crocuses burst out from rocks in the park,
when trees bore crooked yellow pears,
everyday we talked in bars, in cafés, and among Italians.
John slept in an attic in a dirty town south of the river
    Thames.
Since there was no electricity, we put candles into five or six
beer bottles like flowers and lit up our faces a little.
Then we put Donne's poetry and Lewis's pictures into the
    beer-box.
Around that time I was living in a hotel with a rose-patterned
carpet on Brompton Road in South Kensington.
We called this hotel *Roman de la rose.*
Sometimes we bought some roasted chestnuts under the
    moon and went into the *Roman de la rose.*
Together we grieved under the electric light.
We sometimes visited a blind young man who was writing a
    novel
for a proletarian magazine. He was the brave man who
    burned his

beard and eyes lighting fireworks at a celebration party
for the armistice treaty. His wife was most kind and always
hospitable to us.
There was a pub under their apartment. After ten o'clock a
flautist would appear
and play some popular songs, *pyuko, pyuko,*
pyuko. . . . One night we invited him in and had a talk. (He
was planning to play his flute but ended up talking.) Sipping
beer and munching on some sausage, he complained that
he couldn't make much money, for times had changed so
much since
the war.

Translated from the Japanese by Hosea Hirata

At My Sister's Flat in London

EAMON GRENNAN (1941–)

Decent the white flowers on the table
Telling the exact centre, daisies
Their bright eyes open wide
And the table laid for breakfast:
The brown bread coupled to its knife
The butter golden in a green dish
Strong tea brewing in a blue pot
Orange juice brimming a shapely glass.

Things of the ordinary morning world.
This morning luminant under low cloud
Over the tilt solidity of roofs
Their grey slates palely shining,
And in the misted distance the green
Encouraging curvature of trees.

You bless in your own abiding way
Civilities of the gardens parcelled out
To tame grass and the dazzle of roses,
These shrill swifts scything the air,
Keeping their hearts up, in every weather.

Let's Cross

MERLE COLLINS (1950–)

You see me laughing here, is Tottenham have me laughing so
I watching my friend aiming at the West Green Road bakery
thinking bout the hard dough bread and fish paté
and I remembering another time, when she just back in London
from years in Brooklyn, years taking in New York, she tell us,
and those days she holding her handbag tight, tight, tight,
she clutching my arm to breaking as every black man walk up
and her voice rough with the whisper, *Let's cross, let's cross.*

You see me laughing here, is my black sister I watching so
I watching her these days, toe to toe and eyeball
to eyeball with this Tottenham brother,
I listening to her big and bold demanding
Why can't you look where you're going, then?
I hear her add, *git,* as he swings away and I say
Well, look at life. You see, I remembering dem long time days
when I hear her now, crossly shouting, *Let's cross, let's cross.*

You see me laughing here? Is times have me chuckling so.
I can't say I know what brothers in Brooklyn do my sister
but it please me no end to see how after her years back in
        London
I don't have to buy Iodex for my arm when she visit Tottenham
It please me to see how she keep a cross eye on her bag but she
        ain't frighten
how now she back talking to black man like she know him
It please me no end to see how she dodging traffic and
calling out calm and rough like yellow yam, *Let's cross, let's cross.*

Notting Hill Carnival, 1975

ANDREW SALKEY (1928—1995)

Souse, fried fish and mauby,
magical pan, band and float,
costume, swagger and jump-up:
Carnival can't leap the Gulf!

Pick up the Port of Spain display,
complete in the head of the *mas,*
throw it straight across the water
and watch it drop flat and splayed
like a two-day anniversary drunk,
tricked and freaked out as we are,
stepping high, all over the Grove!

Look at the frantic stamp-and-go,
the tugging muddle in the mind,
the heavy hesitation over play,
the forced glinting tone-and-flash,
the tepid menace of the masquerade,
as losers trip and fake bacchanal,
stumbling, up and down the Grove!

Forget the slide of immigration;
simply mime the dreams of exile;
dress the naked pain with images
of history texts, sea and planets
and cross the road with metaphor,
knowing how short ten years are
to squeeze home, into the Grove!

Souse, fried fish and mauby,
magical pan, band and float,
costume, swagger and jump-up:
Carnival can't leap the Gulf!

West London

MATTHEW ARNOLD (1822—1888)

Crouched on the pavement, close by Belgrave Square,
A tramp I saw, ill, moody, and tongue-tied.
A babe was in her arms, and at her side
A girl; their clothes were rags, their feet were bare.

Some labouring men, whose work lay somewhere there,
Passed opposite; she touched her girl, who hied
Across, and begged, and came back satisfied.
The rich she had let pass with frozen stare.

Thought I: "Above her state this spirit towers;
She will not ask of aliens, but of friends,
Of sharers in a common human fate.

She turns from that cold succour, which attends
The unknown little from the unknowing great,
And points us to a better time than ours."

Trafalgar Square at Night

VALERY LARBAUD (1881–1957)

Don't you feel, beggar girl, that it's lovely,
That it's truly delightful to be here
Wandering in this architectural desert
At the heart of the world's largest city, under the
    perpendicular
Stars, the malicious, blinking stars,
Hazy street lamps of the celestial city?
Think no more of your hunger, but amuse yourself
By trying to make out the contours of lions couchant in the
    blue fog,
Beside the terraced black water
Holding the pale reflections of electric globes . . .
Come, I am a good fairy who loves you, and in a moment
You shall have a banquet in your honor and flowers for your
    carriage;
But first let us contemplate for a while
This great nocturnal thing, more beautiful
Than desert or ocean, more beautiful than tropical rivers
Rolling in lunar splendor.
Gaze in silence as you cling to me,
Woman dedicated to the city!

Translated from the French by William Jay Smith

Trafalgar Square

ROBERT BRIDGES (1844–1930)

October, 1917

Fool that I was! my heart was sore,
Yea, sick for the myriad wounded men,
The maim'd in the war: I had grief for each one:
And I came in the gay September sun
To the open smile of Trafalgar Square,
Where many a lad with a limb foredone
Loll'd by the lion-guarded column
That holdeth Nelson statued thereon
Upright in the air.

The Parliament towers, and the Abbey towers,
The white Horseguards and grey Whitehall,
He looketh on all,
Past Somerset House and river's bend
To the pillar'd dome of St. Paul,
That slumbers, confessing God's solemn blessing
On Britain's glory, to keep it ours—
While children true her prowess renew
And throng from the ends of the earth to defend
Freedom and honour—till Earth shall end.

The gentle unjealous Shakespeare, I trow,
In his country grave of peaceful fame
Must feel exiled from life and glow,
If he thinks of this man with his warrior claim,
Who looketh on London as if 't were his own,
As he standeth in stone, aloft and alone,
Sailing the sky, with one arm and one eye.

Paving Stones

RAVI SHANKAR (1975–)

1.

into Marble Arch's
Union Jack's on
shotglasses, woolen
mini Palace guards
crests on waistbands
How much a signifier
in blue and red are
hand-wrapped blurbs
myths, say Tebbit's
when born in Britain
or personal choice
else be photographed

Off the tube
South of the Border:
booties, bootbent
tassel-furled scarves
bulldogs on paddles
satirical rugby mugs—
plastic iconic fetishes
for sterling or Euro
from the sanctioned
Cricket Test:
irrespective of family
support the English side
by the Home Secretary.

2.

the Strand was a pathway
had squared quoins
grain into winnowing baskets
now turned to flats
our dead Queen Mother
Lords and Ladies,
will endeavor to undertake
for the rapid spread
among ewes and cattle
There's TV footage:
on a scale unknown
After that broadcast

Before the Embankment
the Butcher's Arms
flails used to beat
Georgian Tweed Mills
strummed with weavers
had not yet been born.
which noble Baroness
full consular responsibility
of foot-and-mouth disease
in numerous counties?
incineration of the infected
since the Battle of Towton.
most steak jokes bombed.

3.

Noon a snug pub

called the Flying Scud   huddles in a village green

sawdust-thick air souring   jaundiced brass rails

placard calling specials: fried bacon, fried eggs

smoked kipper   grilled tomatoes

kidneys and toast   no white pudding

no soda bread.   George Fame

and the Blue Flames   follows the Troggs

the Honeycombs   on a perspex window jukebox.

The Rod with the Dove   Armillis and Ampulla

the Curtana   the Anointment spoon

the jewels plundered   from three generations

of Indian mughals   who wears them now?

Threadneedle Street

GERTRUDE STEIN (1874–1946)

I am going to conquer. I am going to be flourishing. I am going to be industrious. Please forgive me everything.

Soho: Saturday Night

DANNIE ABSE (1923–)

Always Cain, anonymous amidst the poor,
Abel dead in his eye, and over his damned sore
a khaki muffler, loiters, a fugitive in Soho,
enters The Golden Calf Club and hears Esau,

dishevelled and drunk, cursing kith and kin.
"A mess of pottage!" Esau strokes an unshaven chin
and strikes a marble table-top. Then hairy hands
fidget dolefully, raise up a glass of gin.

Outside, Joseph, dyspnoeic, regards a star
convexing over Dean Street, coughs up a flower
from ruined lungs—rosy petals on his tongue—
recalls the Pit and wounds of many a colour.

Traffic lights change. With tapping white stick
a giant crosses the road between the frantic
taxis. A philistine pimp laughs. Dancing
in The Nude Show Delilah suddenly feels sick.

Ruth, too, the innocent, was gullibly led,
lay down half-clothed on a brassy railing bed
of Mr Boaz of Bayswater. Now, too late, weeps
antiseptic tears, wishes she were dead.

Who goes home? Nebuchadnezzar to the doss-
house where, all night, he'll turn and toss.

Lunchtime, in Soho Square, he munched the grass
and now he howls at strangers as they pass.

In Café Babylon, Daniel, interpreter of dreams,
listens to Belshazzar, a shy lad in his teens:
"A soiled finger moved across the lavatory wall."
Growing up is not so easy as it seems.

Prophets, like tipsters, awaiting the Advent.
Beggar Job, under the flashing advertisement
for toothpaste, the spirochaete in his brain,
groans. Chalks a lurid picture on the pavement.

The Golden Calf closes. Who goes home? All
tourists to Nod; psalmists from their pub crawl;
they leave unshaved Soho to its dawn furnace
of affliction, its wormwood and its gall.

Limping Sonnet

PAUL VERLAINE (1844–1896)

To Ernest Delahaye

It's really very sad that things aren't working out well.
It shouldn't be allowed, to suffer as I am now.
It's really much too much this death of naïve creatures
Who see all their blood flow out beneath their fading eyes.

The smoke and cries of London, that biblical city!
The gas flares up and swims, the signs are painted crimson,
And houses standing there, all shrunken back terribly,
Cause fear as though they were a club of aged women.

The awful past jumps up, it whimpers miaows and bow-wows
Among the dirty pink and yellow fogs of Soho
With its "indeeds" with its "all rights" with its "good evenings."

No really, it's too much a martyr's hopeless torture,
No really, it's too sad, no really things are too bad—
Fire-coal sky hanging over that biblical city!

Translated from the French by Martin Sorrell

Metropolitan

ARTHUR RIMBAUD (1854–1891)

From the indigo straits to the seas of Ossian, on pink and orange sands washed by the vinous sky, crystal boulevards have sprung up, crisscrossing each other, instantly inhabited by poor young families who shop at the fruitmongers'. Nothing grand.——The town!

Fleeing the asphalt desert with mists spreading in ghastly bands across the sky which curves upwards, recedes and descends, composed of the most sinister black smoke given off by a mourning ocean, helmets, wheels, boats and horses' croups.——Battle!

Look up: this arched wooden bridge; the last vegetable gardens of Samaria; those flushed face-masks under a lantern whipped by the cold night; the foolish water spirit in a loud dress down by the river; those luminous skulls amid the rows of peas—and other phantasmagoria—the countryside.

Roads bordered by railings and walls scarcely able to keep back the trees, and hideous flowers that could be called sweethearts and sisters, Damascus damning with languor, possessions of fairytale Rhenish, Japanese and Guarani aristocracies, willing still to embrace the music of the ancients—and there are inns which have already closed their doors forever, there are princesses, and if you're not already overwhelmed, there's stargazing.——The sky.

That morning when you wrestled with Her amid the glaring shards of snow, those green lips, the freezing cold, the black flags and the blue rays, and the purple perfumes of the polar sun.——Your strength.

NOTE: *The title refers to the London Metropolitan Line, the original section of the London Underground, which was already up and running while Rimbaud was in London. This was the first "underground" in the world, even though parts of it were still overground. My own contribution to Rimbaud mythography is the suggestion that he may have been remembering not only what is still known as the Metropolitan Line (the architecture is unchanged in part), but also a famous drawing of it by Gustave Doré, which he could have seen in the New Bond Street gallery exclusively devoted to the work of Doré.——Anthony Rudolf*

Translated from the French by Anthony Rudolf and Ros Schwartz

The British Museum

MIROSLAV HOLUB (1923–1998)

To the tune of "Bolero,"
any ark
will be ruined
once, the trilingual
Rosetta Stone will be broken, steles of Halicarnassus
will turn to dust, sandstone Assyrian spirits
with eagle heads will shyly take off,
the carved man-head lions of Ashursirpolis will croak,
the last red-granite hand of the Colossus of Thebes
will drop off, the Indian supergod Harikaru
will cover his onyx eyes, the Rhind mathematical scrolls
will catch fire, the suspended Zen poems will evaporate,
and the green hellish judge from the Ming dynasty will whine.

For the time of stone is meted out
and so is the time of myth.

Only genes are eternal,
from body to body,
from one breed to another breed,
on Southampton Row
in fact
you find walking genetic codes of Egyptian mummies,
deoxyribonucleic acid of the man from Gebelin,
hereditary traits of the man from Lindow,
whose bodily receptacle, cut in half by a bulldozer,
successfully swells under a glass bell,
in Bloomsbury, in fact, you find

all the eternity of the world rushing around
buying black flowers
for the Last Judgment, less Last
than a midnight hotdog.

So the British Museum is not to be found
in the British Museum.
The British Museum is in us,
quite in the middle,
quite at the bottom.

Translated from the Czech by David Young and Dana Hábová

St Martin-in-the-Fields

HERBERT LOMAS (1924–)

City churches aren't always easy
to pray in: there may be someone buffing up brasses
pianissimo, insistently, with cheesy
breath and a polish of rage behind their glasses,
sending almost tangible meditations
to distract our straggly congregations.

Or visitors delicately boggle at the faithful patients,
Guide Book in hand, not expecting religion
in architecture like this. Outside, the pigeons
drop little pats of white on assembled nations;
inside we pray, uneasily wondering:
whoever it is up there, is he listening?

Yet here bums in a blue-chinned Greek-looking worshipper,
pockets stuffed with evening newspapers, coat
flapping, and grabs his God by the throat:
he prays precipitately, wagging his head—a pew-gripper
pointing out to an old employer—what?
Is it horses? A tip flopped? A reproach or not?

And suddenly I'm in it: his grace has snatched
me out: over the altar the angels' faces
break the wood: they're reaching down with fact,
listening, embracing, swooping, and I'm hatched:
a broad white shell of completeness
has widened and cracked:
I'm open to sweetness.

Parliament Hill Fields

SYLVIA PLATH (1932—1963)

On this bald hill the new year hones its edge.
Faceless and pale as china
The round sky goes on minding its business.
Your absence is inconspicuous;
Nobody can tell what I lack.

Gulls have threaded the river's mud bed back
To this crest of grass. Inland, they argue,
Settling and stirring like blown paper
Or the hands of an invalid. The wan
Sun manages to strike such tin glints

From the linked ponds that my eyes wince
And brim; the city melts like sugar.
A crocodile of small girls
Knotting and stopping, ill-assorted, in blue uniforms,
Opens to swallow me. I'm a stone, a stick,

One child drops a barrette of pink plastic;
None of them seem to notice.
Their shrill, gravelly gossip's funneled off.
Now silence after silence offers itself.
The wind stops my breath like a bandage.

Southward, over Kentish Town, an ashen smudge
Swaddles roof and tree.
It could be a snowfield or a cloudbank.

I suppose it's pointless to think of you at all.
Already your doll grip lets go.

The tumulus, even at noon, guards its black shadow:
You know me less constant,
Ghost of a leaf, ghost of a bird.
I circle the writhen trees. I am too happy.
These faithful dark-boughed cypresses

Brood, rooted in their heaped losses.
Your cry fades like the cry of a gnat.
I lose sight of you on your blind journey,
While the heath grass glitters and the spindling rivulets
Unspool and spend themselves. My mind runs with them,

Pooling in heel-prints, fumbling pebble and stem.
The day empties its images
Like a cup or a room. The moon's crook whitens,
Thin as the skin seaming a scar.
Now, on the nursery wall,

The blue night plants, the little pale blue hill
In your sister's birthday picture start to glow.
The orange pompons, the Egyptian papyrus
Lights up. Each rabbit-eared
Blue shrub behind the glass

Exhales an indigo nimbus,
A sort of cellophane balloon.
The old dregs, the old difficulties take me to wife.
Gulls stiffen to their chill vigil in the drafty half-light;
I enter the lit house.

North Kensington

JOSEPH BRODSKY (1940–1996)

The rustle of an *Irish Times* harried by the wind along
railway tracks to a depot long abandoned,
the crackle of dead wormwood, heralding autumn,
a gray tongue of water close by gums of brick.
How I love these sounds—the sounds of aimless
but continuing life, which for long enough
have been sufficient, aside from the crunch of
my own weighty tread on the gravel. And I fling a bolt skyward.
Only a mouse comprehends the delights of waste ground—
a rusting rail, discarded metal pins,
slack wire, reduced to a husky C-sharp,
the defeat of time in the face of metal.
All beyond repair, no further use.
You can only asphalt it over or blast
it clean off the face of the earth, used by now
to grimacing concrete stadia and their bawling crowds.
Then the mouse will come. Slowly, no rush,
out into the middle of the field, tiny as the soul
is in relation to the flesh, and, raising its
little snout, aghast, will shriek, "What is this place?"

The Peacock in Walpole Park, Ealing

AMARJIT CHANDAN (1946–)

The heart sinks when the peacock screams
The night bleeds pierced with its cries

The heart sinks when the peacock screams
The colour laughs and then wails

The heart sinks when the peacock screams
The body shivers and the world rejoices

The heart sinks when the peacock screams
It yearns for mango flowers lost long ago

The heart sinks when the peacock screams
It rains incessantly, it never stops

The heart sinks when the peacock screams
Trying to slake the thirst burning in its chest

The heart sinks when the peacock screams
Weighing its wings in the sweet prison

Everybody saw it in its cage
Moaning and dancing

Translated from the Punjabi by Amin Mughal, John Welch, and the poet

Smelling the End of Green July

PETER YATES (1909–1976)

Smelling the end of green July
I entered through spiked-gates a London park
To grill my body in the sun,
And to untie thought's parcel of pure dark
Under the blue gaze of the candid sky.

The air was heavy, without breath;
The asphalt paths gave off a hollow ring;
And wearing haloes of shrill birds
The statues watched the flowers withering,
And leaves curl up for Summer's rusty death.

O zoo-like sameness of all parks!
The grasses lick the railings of wrought-iron,
And chains clink in the shrubbery
As Summer roaring like a shabby lion
Claws at the meaning of the human marks.

I saw the tops of buses wheel
Geranium flashes over pigeon-walls;
And heard the rocket-cries of children
Fly upwards, bursting where the water calls,
And scissors sunlight with a glint of steel.

The wings of slowly dripping light
Pulled boats across a swan-enlightened lake;
And near youth's skipping-ropes of joy

I felt the strings of my old parcel break,
Spilling its cold abstractions with delight.

I watched the games of life begun
Among dead matches, droppings of the birds;
And left thought's parcel on a bench
While I relearned the flight of singing words
Under the blowlamp kisses of the sun.

FROM *"District and Circle"*

SEAMUS HEANEY (1939–)

So deeper into it, crowd-swept, strap-hanging,
My lofted arm a-swivel like a flail,
My father's glazed face in my own waning
And craning . . .
                              Again the growl
Of shutting doors, the jolt and one-off treble
Of iron on iron, then a long centrifugal
Haulage of speed through every dragging socket.

And so by night and by day to be transported
Through galleried earth with them, the only relict
Of all that I belonged to, hurtled forward,
Reflecting in a window mirror-backed
By blasted weeping rock-walls.
                              Flicker-lit.

FIRE

London

WILLIAM BLAKE (1757–1827)

I wander thro' each charter'd street,
Near where the charter'd Thames does flow,
And mark in every face I meet
Marks of weakness, marks of woe.

In every cry of every Man,
In every Infant's cry of fear,
In every voice, in every ban,
The mind-forg'd manacles I hear.

How the Chimney-sweeper's cry
Every black'ning Church appalls;
And the hapless Soldier's sigh
Runs in blood down Palace walls.

But most thro' midnight streets I hear
How the youthful Harlot's curse
Blasts the new born Infant's tear,
And blights with plagues the Marriage hearse.

FROM Annus Mirabilis

JOHN DRYDEN (1631–1700)

The powder blows up all before the fire:
    Th' amazed flames stand gather'd on a heap;
And from the precipices brinck retire,
    Afraid to venture on so large a leap.

Thus fighting fires a while themselves consume,
    But straight, like *Turks,* forc'd on to win or die,
They first lay tender bridges of their fume,
    And o'r the breach in unctuous vapours flie.

Part stays for passage till a gust of wind
    Ships o'r their forces in a shining sheet:
Part, creeping under ground, their journey blind,
    And, climbing from below, their fellows meet.

Thus, to some desart plain, or old wood side,
    Dire night-hags come from far to dance their round:
And o'r brode Rivers on their fiends they ride,
    Or sweep in clowds above the blasted ground.

No help avails: for, *Hydra*-like, the fire,
    Lifts up his hundred heads to aim his way.
And scarce the wealthy can one half retire,
    Before he rushes in to share the prey.

FROM *"New Craas Massakah"*

LINTON KWESI JOHNSON (1952–)

to the memory of the fourteen dead

first di comin
an di goin
in and out af di pawty

di dubbin
an di rubbin
an di rackin to di riddim

di dancing
an di scankin
and di pawty really swingin

den di crash
an di bang
an di flames staat fi trang

di heat
an di smoke
an di people staat fi choke

di screamin
an di cryin
an di diein in di fyah . . .

.   .   .   .
fi know seh dem kine a ting deh
couda hapn to we

inna disya Great Britn
inna Landan tiddey
and a few get frightn
an a few get subdue
almost evrybady ad to sympahtise
wid di love wans of di inju and di ded
far disya massakah mek we come fi realise
it couda be mi
it couda be yu
ar wan a fi wi pickney dem
who fell victim to di terrah by nite

.   .   .   .

is a hellava someting fi true yu know
wat a terrible price wi haffi pay dow, mah
jus fi live a likkle life
jus fi struggle fi suvive
evryday is jus worries an struggle an strife
imagine, soh much young people
cut awf before dem prime
before di twilite a dem time
widout reazn nar rhyme
kyastin dis shadow af gloom owevah wi life

look how di police an di press
yry dem despahret bes
fi put a stap to wi ques fi di trute
yu membah? fus dem seh it could be arson
den dem seh parhaps nat
fus dem seh a fyah-bam
den dem seh maybe nat
dem imply it couda white
dem imply it couda black

who rispance fi di attack
gense doze innocent young blacks

.   .   .   .

first di comin
an di going
in an out af di pawty

di dubbin
an a rubbin
an a rackin to di riddim

di dancing
an di scankin
an di pawty really swingin

di lawfin
an di taakin
an di stylin in di pawty

di movin
an a grooving
an di dancing to di disco

di jokin
an di jiving
an di joy af di pawty

den di crash
an di bang
an di flames staat fi trang

di heat

an di smoke
an di people staat fi choke

di screamin
an di cryin
an di diein in di fyah

di panic
an di pushin
an di borin through di fyah

di runnin
an di jumpin
an di flames dem risin highah

di weepin
an di moanin
o di harrow af di fyah

"Oh LONDON I once more to thee do speak"

MARY ADAMS (Seventeenth Century)

Oh LONDON I once more to thee do speak
    Because thy Pride has made my Heart to ake
To See thy Pride and eke Abomination
    Which causeth the Lord to send such Visitations,
As Plague and Pestilence, Fire and Sword,
    Because thou will not hearken to his Word,
Which cut off Thousands in a little time,
    Methinks it should not so soon be out of mind;
Also the great Fire which raged up and down,
    Throughout the City, till 'twas almost consum'd
That Thousands were left without habitations;
    Oh! Do not forget the Lord in such great visitations.
I must confess the Judgments were very great,
    But to what End I to you must relate,
That you should see by those his Visitations
    Your horrid Sins and great Abominations
What Pride and Pleasures are found in this great City,
    With Oaths and other great Abominations, which makes
      me pity
To see the Sad and Deplorable State thou art in
    Which will cause the Lord more Plagues on thee to send.
What Sins were found in Sodom and Gomorrah,
    Also the Great Cruelty of Pharaoh
That is not found in this Wicked Generation?
    Therefore repent with speed, lest it prove your Damnation.

FROM *"To Bryher [1]"*

H.D. (1886–1961)

for Karnak 1923
from London 1942

Pompeii has nothing to teach us,
we know crack of volcanic fissure,
slow flow of terrible lava,

pressure on heart, lungs, the brain
about to burst its brittle case
(what the skull can endure!):

over us, Apocryphal fire,
under us, the earth sway, dip of a floor,
slope of a pavement

where men roll, drunk
with a new bewilderment,
sorcery, bedevilment:

the bone-frame was made for
no such shock knit within terror,
yet the skeleton stood up to it:

the flesh? it was melted away,
the heart burnt out, dead ember,
tendons, muscles shattered, outer husk dismembered,

yet the frame held:
we passed the flame: we wonder
what saved us? what for?

Still Falls the Rain

DAME EDITH SITWELL (1887–1964)

The Raids, 1940. Night and Dawn

Still falls the Rain—
Dark as the world of man, black as our loss—
Blind as the nineteen hundred and forty nails
Upon the Cross.

Still falls the Rain
With a sound like the pulse of the heart that is changed to
    the hammer-beat
In the Potter's Field, and the sound of the impious feet

On the Tomb:
            Still falls the Rain
In the Field of Blood where the small hopes breed and the
    human brain
Nurtures its greed, that worm with the brow of Cain.

Still falls the Rain
At the feet of the Starved Man hung upon the Cross.
Christ that each day, each night, nails there, have mercy
    on us—
On Dives and on Lazarus:
Under the Rain the sore and the gold are as one.

Still falls the Rain—
Still falls the Blood from the Starved Man's wounded Side:
He bears in His Heart all wounds—those of the light that
    died,

The last faint spark
In the self-murdered heart, the wounds of the sad
    uncomprehending dark,
The wounds of the baited bear—
The blind and weeping bear whom the keepers beat
On his helpless flesh . . . the tears of the hunted hare.

Still falls the Rain—
Then—O Ile leape up to my God: who pulles me doune—
See, see where Christ's blood streames in the firmament:
It flows from the Brow we nailed upon the tree
Deep to the dying, to the thirsting heart
That holds the fires of the world—dark-smirched with pain
As Caesar's laurel crown.

Then sounds the voice of One who like the heart of man
Was once a child who among beasts has lain—
"Still do I love, still shed my innocent light, my Blood, for thee."

An Air on London and Paris

JEAN COCTEAU (1889–1963)

It must be red roses
Torrential under heaven
Or certainly a curtain stirring
That hides the essential

It must be torrential rain
Something definitive
That bears away heaven's tablets
Engraved with penknife slashes

It must be roses roses
Extraordinary roses
Where one can make out
The very mechanism of the nerves

Roses exquisitely varicose
And with nerves prepuces calyxes
Perfumed a kind of vow

It must be the red roses
On the table-cloth of Oscar Wilde
Sent expressly into one's hovel
At the pleasure of some duchess

Huge huge stupidity
In the style of an icon
Or pepper Asians put
To spice up rice
The dead of London and Paris

To dine on woodcocks and trout
On the champagne of Russian princes
That's how cities noted
By Nostradamus were destroyed.

NOTE: *This poem was written by Cocteau on the title page of an English review called* Yellowjacket, *an issue dated 1939. Cocteau wrote poems in response to both World Wars. Max Jacob, his poet friend, was murdered by the Nazis.* —Stephen Margulies

Translated from the French by Stephen Margulies

FROM *"Poem in Three Parts"*

DAVID YOUNG (1936–)

A London Saturday. One year ago.
C. and I walk through the V and A,
happy to study replicas. Half a mile off
the Irish Republican Army
has car-bombed a street next to Harrods.
Blood
and broken glass
and a strange hush. Elsewhere,
a waiter drizzles oil on a salad.
In our flat near Baker Street
my wife reads, turning pages.
Bright fibers rim a shawl. Pink candles
infuse a churchy gloom.
Smell of ammonia from somewhere.
A guard yawns. A madman squints.
Hung by its feet,
a pheasant sways in a butcher's window.
Leaves blow in the park.
Time bleeds.
Holly bushes glitter.

Once again I do not know
how this can be turned into words
and held steady
even for a moment:
it slides across your eye
and flickers in your mind.

You look up from the page.

The Burning of Parliament, 1834

STEVE GEHRKE (1971–)

After J. M. W. Turner

He can see the flames settled deep in their faces,
        that reflective urge he's noticed lately in the skin,
all the onlookers tipsy in the half-shells of their boats,
        some praying, some clasping jugs of wine,
as they turn towards Parliament, rooting themselves

into the mud, the strangled chain of each anchor turning
        spinal underneath like the smoke that unknots
continually above, anchoring the sky to the dead,
        the consumptive, industrious smoke, marbled
with ashes and grains of exploded glass, on its way to convert

the screams of the dying into rain. Walking out along the dock-
        boards of his vision, a glob of yellow
on his palette, like a coin he dips into with his brush,
        as if the whole color might be spent
on the extravagance of flames, Turner feels the fire

become a small glow that fills him as he paints,
        like a secret growing in importance,
as if, when he lets it back out into the landscape,
        it might restore the holy mystery, might end
the authority of shape. Palette knife, mineral spirits dissolving

in a solvent cup, umbrella pluming from the mud,
        each brushstroke a flamboyant wound, the way,

in his father's barber-shop, for the first time being shaved,
      among water froth and steam, the gleaming metal,
soap stirred onto a lather brush, the scissors chirping like a beak,

he felt, as punishment for some forgotten sin, his father
      twitch his wrist, just slightly, to make
a nick into his skin, the crushed petals of his blood
      darkening a cloth, the moment already clotted
in his face. Though now, as his father's gesture renews itself

as paint, as epileptic flinches on the canvas,
      each motion quick as flipping a watch lid
closed, the past awakens into candle-dust and hue,
      a match-stroke grown into the flickering landscape,
so that, standing there, with the wind-caught flames slurred

above the bay, he begins to see the present as a shore
      from which to watch the past disintegrate,
the way, bored, he traced his outline onto the steam-
      fogged window of his father's shop,
then let the cold leak in, and breathless, watched himself

evaporate, his ghost-self trapped in the suffocating
      glass, as he imagined being tossed
through the window of his own body, the body
      shattering behind him. And doesn't
freedom, at last, have to be like that—fracturing, bold—

the self a border we cross and cross into flames, which,
      even now, are less a destruction
than the eviction of what lay, for years, ripening within,
      each board erupting with the sizzle passed
down through the wick of his veins, the coin-glint

from Parliament's chambers swirled into the paint,
  as if its arguments and pleas, the deep red
gloves pulled on by the executioning judge could
  be sewn together in the blaze. Once, with sleight
of hand, his father polished a coin into a cloth,

then tossed the bankrupt fabric in the air, as if the money
  might lay vaulted in the steam, though
at the time, confused, awe-struck in his father's light,
  he felt as if the coin might be locked
in him, hard and inextinguishable, radiating beneath

the skin, erupting, like the spirit, through the pores,
  though later, sweeping—now the image
slides out behind the paint, as Parliament collapses
  in a heap—he found the coin, still
smoldering, beneath the mound of the day's forsaken hair.

A London Fête

COVENTRY PATMORE (1823–1896)

All night fell hammers, shock on shock;
With echoes Newgate's granite clang'd:
The scaffold built, at eight o'clock
They brought the man out to be hang'd.
Then came from all the people there
A single cry, that shook the air;
Mothers held up their babes to see,
Who spread their hands, and crow'd for glee;
Here a girl from her vesture tore
A rag to wave with, and join'd the roar;
There a man, with yelling tired,
Stopp'd, and the culprit's crime inquired;
A sot, below the doom'd man dumb,
Bawl'd his health in the world to come;
These blasphemed and fought for places;
Those, half-crush'd, cast frantic faces,
To windows, where, in freedom sweet,
Others enjoy'd the wicked treat.
At last, the show's black crisis pended;
Struggles for better standings ended;
The rabble's lips no longer curst,
But stood agape with horrid thirst;
Thousands of breasts beat horrid hope;
Thousands of eyeballs, lit with hell,
Burnt one way all, to see the rope
Unslacken as the platform fell.
The rope flew tight; and then the roar
Burst forth afresh; less loud, but more

Confused and affrighting than before.
A few harsh tongues for ever led
The common din, the chaos of noises,
But ear could not catch what they said.
As when the realm of the damn'd rejoices
At winning a soul to its will,
That clatter and clangour of hateful voices
Sicken'd and stunn'd the air, until
The dangling corpse hung straight and still.
The show complete, the pleasure past,
The solid masses loosen'd fast:
A thief slunk off, with ample spoil,
To ply elsewhere his daily toil;
A baby strung its doll to a stick;
A mother praised the pretty trick;
Two children caught and hang'd a cat;
Two friends walk'd on, in lively chat;
And two, who had disputed places,
Went forth to fight, with murderous faces.

London Stone

RUDYARD KIPLING (1865–1936)

When you come to London Town,
    (Grieving—grieving!)
Bring your flowers and lay them down
    At the Place of Grieving.

When you come to London Stone,
    (Grieving—grieving!)
Bow your head and mourn your own,
    With the others grieving.

For those minutes, let it wake—
    (Grieving—grieving!)
All the empty heart and ache
    That isn't cured by grieving.

For those minutes, tell no lie:—
    (Grieving—grieving!)
"Grave, this is thy victory;
    And the sting of Death is grieving."

Where's our help, from Earth or Heaven?
    (Grieving—grieving!)
To comfort us for what we've given,
    And only gained the grieving.

Heaven's too far and Earth too near,
    (Grieving—grieving!)
But our neighbour's standing here,
    Grieving as we're grieving.

What's his burden every day?
    (Grieving—grieving!)
Nothing man can count or weigh,
    But loss and Love's own grieving.

What's the tie betwixt us two
    (Grieving—grieving!)
That must last our whole lives through?
"As I suffer so do you."
    That may ease the grieving.

FROM *"In Nunhead Cemetery"*

CHARLOTTE MEW (1869–1928)

There is something horrible about a flower;
    This, broken in my hand, is one of those
He threw in just now: it will not live another hour;
    There are thousands more: you do not miss a rose.

One of the children hanging about
    Pointed at the whole dreadful heap and smiled
This morning, after THAT was carried out;
    There is something terrible about a child.

We were like children, last week, in the Strand;
    That was the day you laughed at me
Because I tried to make you understand
    The cheap, stale chap I used to be
    Before I saw the things you made me see.

This is not a real place; perhaps by-and-by
    I shall wake——I am getting drenched with all this rain:
To-morrow I will tell you about the eyes of the Crystal
    Palace train
        Looking down on us, and you will laugh and I shall see
            what you see again.

        Not here, not now. We said "Not yet
        Across our low stone parapet
    Will the quick shadows of the sparrows fall."

        But still it was a lovely thing
        Through the grey months to wait for Spring

With the birds that go a-gypsying
In the parks till the blue seas call.
     And next to these, you used to care
     For the lions in Trafalgar Square,
Who'll stand and speak for London when her bell of Judgment
     tolls—
     And the gulls at Westminster that were
     The old sea-captains' souls.
To-day again the brown tide splashes, step by step, the river
     stair,
     And the gulls are there!
          .   .   .   .

We should have stood on the gulls' black cliffs and heard the sea
     And seen the moon's white track,
I would have called, you would have come to me
     And kissed me back.

You have never done that: I do not know
     Why I stood staring at your bed
And heard you, though you spoke so low,
     But could not reach your hands, your little head.
There was nothing we could not do, you said,
     And you went, and I let you go!

Now I will burn you back, I will burn you through,
     Though I am damned for it we two will lie
     And burn, here where the starlings fly
     To these white stones from the wet sky—;
     Dear, you will say this is not I—
It would not be you, it would not be you!

If for only a little while
    You will think of it you will understand,
      If you will touch my sleeve and smile
    As you did that morning in the Strand
        I can wait quietly with you
        Or go away if you want me to—
    God! What is God? but your face has gone and your hand!
        Let me stay here too.

     .   .   .   .   .   .

I shall stay here: here you can see the sky;
The houses in the street are much too high;
    There is no one left to speak to there;
    Here they are everywhere,
And just above them fields and fields of roses lie—
If he would dig it all up again they would not die.

A Refusal to Mourn the Death, by Fire, of a Child in London

DYLAN THOMAS (1914–1953)

Never until the mankind making
Bird beast and flower
Fathering and all humbling darkness
Tells with silence the last light breaking
And the still hour
Is come of the sea tumbling in harness

And I must enter again the round
Zion of the water bead
And the synagogue of the ear of corn
Shall I let pray the shadow of a sound
Or sow my salt seed
In the least valley of sackcloth to mourn

The majesty and burning of the child's death.
I shall not murder
The mankind of her going with a grave truth
Nor blaspheme down the stations of the breath
With any further
Elegy of innocence and youth.

Deep with the first dead lies London's daughter,
Robed in the long friends,
The grains beyond age, the dark veins of her mother,
Secret by the unmourning water
Of the riding Thames.
After the first death, there is no other.

Deceptions

PHILIP LARKIN (1922–1985)

Of course I was drugged, and so heavily I did not regain my
consciousness till the next morning. I was horrified to discover
that I had been ruined, and for some days I was inconsolable,
and cried like a child to be killed or sent back to my aunt.
—Mayhew, *London Labour and the London Poor*

Even so distant, I can taste the grief,
Bitter and sharp with stalks, he made you gulp.
The sun's occasional print, the brisk brief
Worry of wheels along the street outside
Where bridal London bows the other way,
And light, unanswerable and tall and wide,
Forbids the scar to heal, and drives
Shame out of hiding. All the unhurried day
Your mind lay open like a drawer of knives.

Slums, years, have buried you. I would not dare
Console you if I could. What can be said,
Except that suffering is exact, but where
Desire takes charge, readings will grow erratic?
For you would hardly care
That you were less deceived, out on that bed,
Than he was, stumbling up the breathless stair
To burst into fulfilment's desolate attic.

A Metropolitan Christmas

London

EUGENIO MONTALE (1896–1981)

Mistletoe, from childhood a hanging cluster
of faith and hoar-frost over your washstand
and the oval mirror which your shepherd-curls
now shadow among the paper saints and photographs
of boys slipped helter-skelter into
the frame; an empty decanter,
small glasses of ashes and rinds,
the lights of Mayfair; then, at a crossroads,
souls and bottles which could not be opened—
no longer war or peace; the final whirr
of a pigeon unable to follow you
on the escalator which slides you down . . .

Translated from the Italian by Charles Wright

The Sky Comes Down to Earth

JON THOMPSON (1959–)

How could we have forgotten that this was always
going to happen?
—Ian McEwan on the attack on London, July 7, 2005

Leaving streets relics of former selves   the aftermath
is of silence & the dirge of sirens.   Annihilation of the
familiar / stillness / warm dream of heaven. We do   wonder
at the corpses of empire   fallen   "the multiplying
villainies of nature do swarm upon us." Grotesque imitation
of the battlefield / the looking-glass   has shattered &
shards of reflection—bits of a blue sky—litter the
streets.   *Were't not more than my Tongue can tell; I thus
would pray*   In the rubble, country and city disavow
all cousinly kinship. No longer any way to go from here to
there, & no way of going back   "We but teach / Bloody
instructions, which, being taught, return / To plague the
inventor."   Whispered words silent words last words: "I
wanted only that . . ." /
Your question, your answer

Mourning and Melancholia

A. ALVAREZ (1929–)

His face was blue, on his fingers
Flecks of green. "This is my father,"
I thought. Stiff and unwieldy
He stared out of my sleep. The parlourmaid
Smiled from the bed with his corpse,
Her chapped lips thin and welcoming.
In the next room her albino child
Kept shouting, shouting; I had to put him down
Like a blind puppy. "Death from strangulation
By persons known." I kept the clipping
In my breast-pocket where it burns and burns,
Stuck to my skin like phosphorus.

I wake up struggling, silent, undersea
Light and a single thrush
Is tuning up. You sleep, the baby sleeps,
The town is dead. Foxes are out on the Heath;
They sniff the air like knives.
A hawk turns slowly over Highgate, waiting.
This is the hidden life of London. Wild.

Three years back my father's corpse was burnt,
His ashes scattered. Now I breathe him in
With the grey morning air, in and out.
In out. My heart bumps steadily
Without pleasure. The air is thick with ash.
In out. I am cold and powerless. His face
Still pushes sadly into mine. He's disappointed.
I've let him down, he says. Now I'm cold like him.
Cold and untameable. Will have to be put down.

A Linden Tree in a Whitechapel Street

AVRAM NOCHUM STENCL (1897–1983)

Not in the countryside in a green field,
Spreading its branches wide,
With a flock of sheep sheltering under it,
With the shepherd at their side.

Not rooted in soft country soil,
With green fields all round,
But in a Whitechapel street,
In hard asphalted ground.

With his legs bound and his wings spread,
But never able to rise and fly,
The tree stands in this Whitechapel street.
And so do I.

Then suddenly the whole street is aflame.
There's a bird singing in the tree.
And somehow it seems to be singing
Also to me.

Translated from the Yiddish by Joseph Leftwich

AIR

FROM *"The Firebird"*

PRISCILLA SNEFF (1956–)

Night planes over England, night of wings, night of
Light shows over megaliths; O
My soul,
The desire and the pursuit of
The whole.
The mere vision:
The ticking and integral stone, set
Still in its open tomb, quick
And dreaming voluptuous dreams:
Explosion.

∞

O Love is absurd O gilded flack
Each sonnet.

∞

Something I have seen in London——Love-
In-Illness under cool, taut linen;
Something I can't dream of: winged peace;
Something——the nervy world burning through nightmare——
Troubles my heartstrings. Something . . .

∞

I wait in the city for something——vision——and see dream-
Shapes, flapping and dim-lit, but they are only dreamt.

See a hazy flock, sleep-fraught and night-flying, of huge, light,
Mechanical birds. See the delicate slim-limbed primates
Traversing the shattered curbs in silverish streamlets. Greet
One visitant after another, delightedly!, but never on the first sight.

Cave. Cave.
And who *is* this croaks, "My dear, my dear,
I shall carry you over the lintel and through the white doors."

London

RANDALL JARRELL (1914–1965)

The wind wore me north, London I left a year.
—When the wind blows, boy, the bough is bare.—
When I came south in summer like a goose,
Leaves were more than I found left to lose.

I came to London, what did I find there?
I found my house full and my cupboard bare,
They sold my skillets and they stole my knives,
My wives have husbands and my husbands wives.

London, London, O where are you gone?
—No place is, child, man calls his own.
He tumbles all unwilling from the womb,
He reaches for a breast and gets a bone;

He calls his father God, his mother wife,
Of all the letters he knows only *I*.
And yet at last, man, you must learn to live,
Though you want nothing but to die.

Rain Journal: London: June 65

LEE HARWOOD (1939–)

sitting naked together
on the edge of the bed
drinking vodka

this is my first real love scene

your body so good
your eyes sad love stars

but John
now when we're miles apart
the come-down from mountain visions
and the streets all raining
and me in the back of a shop
making free phone calls to you

what can we do?

crackling telephone wires shadow me
and this distance haunts me
and yes—I am miserable
and lost without you

whole days spent
remaking your face
the sound of your voice
the feel of your shoulder

An Umbrella from Piccadilly

JAROSLAV SEIFERT (1901–1986)

If you're at your wits' end with love
try falling in love again—
say, with the Queen of England.
Why not?
Her features are on every postage stamp
of that ancient kingdom.
But if you were to ask her
for a date in Hyde Park
you can bet on it
you'd wait in vain.

If you've any sense at all
you'll wisely tell yourself:
Why of course, I know:
it's raining in Hyde Park today.

When he was coming back from England
my son bought me in London's Piccadilly
an elegant umbrella.
Whenever necessary
I now have above my head
my own small sky
which may be black
but in its tensioned wire spokes
God's mercy may be flowing like
electric current.

I open my umbrella even when it's not raining,
as a canopy

over the volume of Shakespeare's sonnets
I carry with me in my pocket.

But there are moments when I am frightened
even by the sparkling bouquet of the universe.
Outstripping its beauty
it threatens us with its infinity
and that is all too similar
to the sleep of death.

It also threatens us with the void and frostiness
of its thousands of stars
which at night delude us
with their gleam.

The one we have named Venus
is downright terrifying.
Its rocks are still on the boil
and like gigantic waves of the sea
mountains are rising up
and burning sulphur falls.

We always ask where hell is.
It is there!

But what use is a fragile umbrella
against the universe?
Besides I don't even carry it.
I have enough of a job
to walk along,
clinging close to the ground

as a nocturnal moth in daytime
to the coarse bark of a tree.

All my life I have sought the paradise
that used to be here,
whose traces I have found
only on women's lips
and in the curves of their skin
when it was warm with love.

All my life I've longed
for freedom.
At last I've discovered the door
that leads to it.
It is death.

Now that I'm old
some charming woman's face
will sometimes waft between my lashes
and her smile will stir my blood.

Shyly I turn my head
and remember the Queen of England
whose features are on every postage stamp
of that ancient kingdom.
God save the Queen!

Oh yes, I know quite well:
it's raining in Hyde Park today.

Translated from the Czech by Ewald Osers

From My Window

MARY COLERIDGE (1861—1907)

An old man leaning on a gate
Over a London mews—to contemplate—
Is it the sky above—the stones below?
 Is it remembrance of the years gone by,
 Or thinking forward to futurity
That holds him so?

Day after day he stands,
Quietly folded are the quiet hands,
Rarely he speaks.
 Hath he so near the hour when Time shall end,
 So much to spend?
What is it he seeks?

Whate'er he be,
He is become to me
A form of rest.
 I think his heart is tranquil, from it springs
 A dreamy watchfulness of tranquil things,
And not unblest.

Greece

GRETA STODDART (1966—)

Afternoons we have to hide from the heat
where the dog drags his ragged shadow
along the walls. Knives are clean and quiet,
pillows cool, rain remote as tragedy.
In the drawn room as we lie on the verge
of sleep or sex, zapping bad TV,
Chelsea appear and it's like old footage—
men we thought we'd lost forever, a field,
big-dropped Summer rain and that semen
sweet smell that heaves off a certain shrub.
My heart thumps obscurely at the thought of London
as if of a not quite forgotten lover;
and the old song-swell carries from the pitch
like the approach of a massive storm, or myth.

His returne to London

ROBERT HERRICK (1591—1674)

From the dull confines of the drooping West,
To see the day spring from the pregnant East,
Ravisht in spirit, I come, nay more, I flie
To thee, blest place of my Nativitie!
Thus, thus with hallowed foot I touch the ground,
With thousand blessings by thy Fortune crown'd.
O fruitfull Genius! that bestowest here
An everlasting plenty, yeere by yeere.
O *Place!* O *People!* Manners! fram'd to please
All *Nations, Customes, Kindreds, Languages!*
I am a free-born *Roman;* suffer then,
That I amongst you live a Citizen.
London my home is: though by hard fate sent
Into a long and irksome banishment;
Yet since cal'd back; henceforward let me be,
O native countrey, repossest by thee!
For, rather then I'le to the West return,
I'le beg of thee first here to have mine Urn.
Weak I am grown, and must in short time fall;
Give thou my sacred Reliques Buriall.

To the Statues in Poets' Corner, Westminster Abbey

ADRIAN MITCHELL (1932–)

You stony bunch of pockskinned whiteys,
Why kip in here? Who sentenced you?
They are buying postcards of you,
The girls in safety knickers.
Tombfaces, glumbums,
Wine should be jumping out of all your holes,
You should have eyes that roll, arms that knock things over,
Legs that falter and working cocks.
Listen.
On William Blake's birthday we're going to free you,
Blast you off your platforms with a blowtorch full of brandy
And then we'll all stomp over to the Houses of Parliament
And drive them into the Thames with our bananas.

Soho Awakening

MICHAEL HOROVITZ (1935–)

mind's eye opens afresh
from dreamgleam trance

in a pool of petrol
all tones dance

crescent   city   moon
incandescent   through vapours
cuts   back to the arc
of historic   time

sun's spectrum swells
in park enclaves
rainbows plash
off ducks back waters

yea like a sainted medieval spirit
winding fresh flowers
through the black death
dawn   hits   town

piercing skylight and airshaft
through these salvage dumped streets
and bird-brimming squares

even glances down
the underground

FROM *"The Cross Is Gone"*

BEN OKRI (1959–)

We climbed Parliament Hill
Our spirits heaving, our breaths
Quickening, the earth slipping beneath our feet.
The sky quivered with silent birds.
With our ascent we noticed a gathered crowd,
An old woman with a yellow scarf
A black man with a red beret on his bald head
Children playing with strings
A nun with frozen hands
An Irish priest wearing metal-framed glasses
An enormous bible under his arm
A wand in one hand, the string of the red
Kite in the other.

We approached them, holding
Fast to our invisible trail, breathing
Heavily the rarefied air:
And when we gained the hill top
The cross shivered
A strong wind, smelling of incense and radiation,
And disease and French perfume and hidden wars,
Blew over from the distant Thames.

We saw all the world laid out
Before us in the air
A city perceived in a moment's enchantment
Whose history, weighed down with guilt and machines,

Laughed all around us like ghosts
Who do not believe in the existence
Of men.

We saw the city and marvelled.
We dream the city better
Than it dreams itself.

London

YANG LIAN (1955–)

reality is part of my nature
spring has accepted the overflowing green of the dead again
streets   accept more funerals which are blacker yet
   beneath the flowers
red phone boxes in the rain like a warning
time is part of the internal organs   bird voices
open every rusting face on the benches
watching night's eyes a prolonged flying accident
when yet another day is blotted out   London

write out all my madness   lick out all the brown beer's
   froth
the bell's toll in a little bird's brain vibrates like a gloomy verse
   unemployed
the city is part of the word   the most terrifying part of me
showing my insignificance   accepting
blue mildewed sheepskin slip-cover outside the window
sheep meat's memory diligently binding
its own death   dying in   the non-convulsing lens
when between two pages of newsprint is a grave   behind
   the grave is the ocean

Translated from the Chinese by Brian Holton

Battersea Dojo

LAVINIA GREENLAW (1962–)

He lived on lupins steeped in water.
—Pliny the Elder on Protogenes

The hardcore years.
Towers emptied on the strength of a rumour.
For all that, the skyline boomed like a graph.
Inside the walls, money grew on trees.

Barefoot, shaven, crop-headed, a neophyte,
most weeks I had my collar felt.
"Sorry, I thought you were . . ."
A twenty-year-old blur
hauled backwards out of the Ladies.
(Who was it rushed up in the dark to kiss
me, his long-lost boy?)

A hard man with a face in bloom,
sensei liked to play old-fashioned
with his signet ring, conspiracies and heft.
He asked me to pardon his French
as we sat depleted, topping up
on pints of water with a lager chaser.

I learnt to fold myself behind the punch,
retract first then force the twist,
two knuckles raised on a tucked thumb;
to see both ways, to prolong the arc
of a kick in the *kata*'s quick-quick slow.

My dappled forearms noted the force
of my knifehand and rising blocks.
In attack, I was taught to miss by inches.

I was wire.
I drank the blue air.
Towers emptied on the strength of a rumour.

Old-Fashioned Air

TED BERRIGAN (1934–1983)

To Lee Crabtree

I'm living in Battersea, July,
1973, not sleeping, reading
Jet noise throbs building fading
Into baby talking, no, "speechifying"
"Ah wob chuk sh'guh!" Glee.
There's a famous Power Station I can't see
Up the street. Across there is
Battersea Park
I walked across this morning toward
A truly gorgeous radiant flush;
Sun; fumes of the Battersea
Power Station; London Air;
I walked down long avenues with trees
That leant not ungracefully
Over the concrete walk. Wet green lawn
Opened spaciously
Out on either side of me. I saw
A great flock of geese taking their morning walk
Unhurriedly.
I didn't hurry either, Lee.
I stopped & watched them walk back up toward
& down into their lake,
Smoked a Senior Service on a bench
As they swam past me in a long dumb graceful cluttered line,
Then, taking my time, I found my way
Out of that park;

A Gate that was locked. I jumped the fence.
From there I picked up the *London Times,* came home,
Anselm awake in his bed, Alice
Sleeping in mine: I changed
A diaper, read a small poem I'd had
In mind, then thought to write this line:
"Now is Monday morning so, that's a garbage truck I hear,
    not bells" . . .
And we are back where we started from, Lee, you & me,
    alive & well!"

FROM *"Afterwards: Caliban"*

TALVIKKI ANSEL (1962–)

Pears and rue, I walk the London physic
Garden. I knew they would Marry, they
Had the same Eyes; played Chess—I couldn't
Grudge them that. Squares of herbs, regiments
Of onions, parsley against a brick wall,
A wicker Cage for Doves. Why did I leave
The island? So many things I didn't know—
That I would be put out: Fleet Street, beside
The two-headed Infant found in the Thames;
The wicker ports; Garlic stink of People
Pressing close. They kept me until I picked
My scabs too much, slept, Dreamt. It's years ago.
Here: gillie-flower ("Nature's bastard," **carnation**)
Its warm, Breeze-borne scent: cinnamon.

London

EILÉAN NÍ CHUILLEANÁIN (1942–)

At fifty, she misses the breast
That grew in her thirteenth year
And was removed last month. She misses
The small car she drove through the seaside town
And along cliffs for miles. In London
She will not take the tube, is afraid of taxis.

We choose a random bar. She sits by me,
Looking along the jacketed line of men's
Lunchtime backs, drinks her vermouth.
I see her eye slide to the left;
At the counter's end sits a high metal urn.

What are you staring at? That polished curve,
The glint wavering on steel, the features
Of our stranger neighbour distorted.
You can't see it from where you are.
When that streak of crooked light
Goes out, my life is over.

"Thus I wrote in London, musing on my betters"

ROBERT BROWNING (1812–1889)

Thus I wrote in London, musing on my betters,
Poets dead and gone: and lo, the critics cried,
"Out on such a boast!"—as if I dreamed that fetters
Binding Dante, bind up—me! as if true pride
Were not also humble!

               So I smiled and sighed
As I oped your book in Venice this bright morning,
Sweet new friend of mine! and felt the clay or sand
—Whatsoe'er my soil be,—break—for praise or scorning—
Out in grateful fancies—weeds, but weeds expand
Almost into flowers—held by such a kindly hand!

Browning Resolves to Be a Poet

JORGE LUIS BORGES (1899–1986)

In these red London labyrinths
I find that I have chosen
the most curious of human professions,
though given that all are curious, in their way.
Like alchemists
who looked for the philosopher's stone
in elusive quicksilver,
I shall make ordinary words—
the marked cards of the sharper, the people's coinage—
yield up the magic that was theirs
when Thor was inspiration and eruption,
thunder and worship.
In the wording of the day,
I in my turn will say eternal things;
I will try to be not unworthy
of the great echo of Byron.
This dust that is me will be invulnerable.
If a woman shares my love,
my poem will graze the tenth sphere of the concentric
    heavens;
if a woman shrugs off my love,
I will make music out of my misery,
a vast river reverberating through time.
I will live by forgetting myself.
I will be the face I half-see and forget,
I will be Judas who accepts
the blessed destiny of being a traitor,
I will be Caliban in the swamp,

I will be a mercenary dying
without fear or faith,
I will be Polycrates, horrified to see
the ring returned by destiny,
I will be the friend who hates me.
Persia will grant me the nightingale, Rome the sword.
Agonies, masks, and resurrections
will weave and unweave my fate
and at some point I will be Robert Browning.

Translated from the Spanish by Alistair Reid

FROM Aurora Leigh

ELIZABETH BARRETT BROWNING
(1806—1861)

Serene and unafraid of solitude
I worked the short days out,—and watched the sun
On lurid morns or monstrous afternoons

.   .   .   .

Push out through fog with his dilated disk,
And startle the slant roofs and chimney-pots
With splashes of fierce colour. Or I saw
Fog only, the great tawny weltering fog,
Involve the passive city, strangle it
Alive, and draw it off into the void,
Spires, bridges, streets, and squares, as if a spunge
Had wiped out London,—or as noon and night
Had clapped together and utterly struck out
The intermediate time, undoing themselves
In the act. Your city poets see such things
Not despicable. . . .

.   .   .   .

But sit in London at the day's decline,
And view the city perish in the mist
Like Pharaoh's armaments in the deep Red Sea,
The chariots, horsemen, footmen, all the host,
Sucked down and choked to silence—then, surprised
By a sudden sense of vision and of tune,
You feel as conquerors though you did not fight.

By the Statue of King Charles at Charing Cross

LIONEL JOHNSON (1867–1902)

To William Watson

Sombre and rich, the skies;
Great glooms, and starry plains.
Gently the night wind sighs;
Else a vast silence reigns.

The splendid silence clings
Around me: and around
The saddest of all kings
Crowned, and again discrowned.

Comely and calm, he rides
Hard by his own Whitehall:
Only the night wind glides:
No crowds, nor rebels, brawl.

Gone, too, his Court: and yet,
The stars his courtiers are:
Stars in their stations set;
And every wandering star.

Alone he rides, alone,
The fair and fatal king:
Dark night is all his own,
That strange and solemn thing.

Which are more full of fate:
The stars; or those sad eyes?
Which are more still and great:
Those brows; or the dark skies?

Although his whole heart yearn
In passionate tragedy:
Never was face so stern
With sweet austerity.

Vanquished in life, his death
By beauty made amends:
The passing of his breath
Won his defeated ends.

Brief life, and hapless? Nay:
Through death, life grew sublime.
Speak after sentence? Yea:
And to the end of time.

Armoured he rides, his head
Bare to the stars of doom:
He triumphs now, the dead,
Beholding London's gloom.

Our wearier spirit faints,
Vexed in the world's employ:
His soul was of the saints;
And art to him was joy.

King, tried in fires of woe!
Men hunger for thy grace:

And through the night I go,
Loving thy mournful face.

Yet, when the city sleeps;
When all the cries are still:
The stars and heavenly deeps
Work out a perfect will.

Continuous Sky

IAIN SINCLAIR (1943–)

For Lee Harwood

the artist's general disposition to vibrate
—Henry James

a lightgreen coat moves commonly east, un-
inspired, but up for it, a shifty sky with its rouge theatre
stacked in golden curls, cold enough for fingerless gloves, can
you believe "The Poet" is now a wine bar in Mitre Street &
    how does
"6 Irish Oysters with soda bread" (at £7.80) grab you? or
"Seaweed cured Salmon" (at £5.50) backed by a slab of good
Galway taybreadandbutter? the poet is effortlessly divorced
from the poem (like the abuser from mother church). no
solitaries with red notebooks, no silver paint like Stephen
Rodefer's decadent nails. business folk (women included)
drip chardonnay on small round tables. yellow & blue
they have decided will stand as poetry's flag

the motif offers coherence to a fragmented cityscape,
with many obstacles for pedestrians to surmount, keeping
the trek interesting, hurdle fences, tarmac'd mud
carbonized angels in dim recesses, Byzantine tesserae glinting
blood & rubies, unredeemed nimbuses, the run to Cable Street
hobbled, minor league Minories, and it hits me, flashing
to the back story, that "poet" is another way of saying "Irish,"
twisted window-slats that were once blind, only in the
Square Mile are churches heated & open (incensed): *Ralph*

*Clay Esq of Hackney Who in the 65th Year of his Age
closed an honourable and useful Life*

browse nautical charts before swinging left to where
the Seaman's Library used to stand on the corner of
Dock Street, now as you rightly suppose Ludlow Thompson
Residential Sales, blue (again) & old gold (yellow), one-bedroom
apartments of the type that might once have seemed, under
white emulsion, desirable to romantics who read French verse
& liked to blend Gauloises, goat curry and sewage outflow
from the foreshore, Supremes on the jukebox and the
mythical hooting of tugboats on the Thames, all bollocks
like imported sand making a Southend of Tower Bridge.
nothing has gone that was ever here. freakish ceramic cod
the dive with the movie star collages & the sign that leads
the discerning stalker to Wilton's Music Hall with its
astonishing pink door, pomegranate & pineapple panels
the deep eros of purple impinging on blushing labia: BIG
LOVE, shuttered to the blarney screech of Fiona Shaw
emoting the lifeblood out of *The Waste Land*. "the phrases
of the afternoon, or early morning," he wrote, "finally do
make a life full turn." quiet vortices of Bengali kids, post-
economic migrants, unschooled in Wellclose Square, are
shepherded towards asymmetrically lit tower blocks, cloud-
shavings soluble in the still water of the memorial font.
bright chatter, long black coats swishing against the pull
of the L. bones skulls books deals compasses confectionery
loud as third world toothpaste, hospital mosque poverty
pit. getting holding moving on, coming, coming back none
the worse for what has been attempted & abandoned, risk
knowing & not knowing, never knowing when why
& where to turn on your heel, switch off, go home

To the Great Metropolis

ARTHUR HUGH CLOUGH (1819–1861)

Traffic, to speak from knowledge but begun,
I saw, and travelling much, and fashion—Yea,
And if that Competition and Display
Make a great Capital, then thou art one,
One, it may be, unrivalled neath the Sun.
But sovereign symbol of the Great and Good,
True Royalty, and genuine Statesmanhood,
Nobleness, Learning, Piety was none.
If such realities indeed there are
Working within unsignified, 'tis well;
The stranger's fancy of the thing thou art
Is rather truly of a huge Bazaar,
A railway terminus, a gay Hotel,
Anything but a mighty Nation's heart.

Beyond London

LYTTON SMITH (1982–)

I remember the curve and slope
of its streets, beat of streetnames,

a pip-coloured dusk deepening
the Thames. I found another city,

glassfronted and built to the sky,
but of its rivers I know only

the pull and current of Thames,
its bridges are London bridges,

Blackfriars, Southwark, the tread
of steps I have always taken.

This is how London calls me back
to market-sound, to local stone:

At this remove it roots me
for summer afternoons are always

London afternoons and the words
of this city without end sound on.

London

JOHN DAVIDSON (1857–1909)

Athwart the sky a lowly sigh
    From west to east the sweet wind carried;
The sun stood still on Primrose Hill;
    His light in all the city tarried:
The clouds on viewless columns bloomed
Like smouldering lilies unconsumed.

Oh sweetheart, see! how shadowy,
    Of some occult magician's rearing,
Or swung in space of heaven's grace
    Dissolving, dimly reappearing,
Afloat upon ethereal tides
St Paul's above the city rides!

A rumour broke through the thin smoke
    Enwreathing abbey, tower, and palace,
The parks, the squares, the thoroughfares,
    The million-peopled lanes and alleys,
An ever-muttering prisoned storm,
The heart of London beating warm.

Brief Biographies of the Poets

DANNIE ABSE (1923–), Welsh poet, studied medicine at the University of Wales and King's College, London. Before practicing medicine in Soho, he served in the Royal Air Force from 1951 to 1955. Best known for his poetry, Abse has also written fiction and plays.

J. R. ACKERLEY (1896–1967), British poet, is primarily known for his autobiography, *My Father and Myself,* and eccentric novels, such as *My Dog Tulip.* His experiences as a captured officer in World War I provided material for his play, *The Prisoners of War.* From 1935 to 1939 Ackerley worked as literary editor for the BBC weekly *Listener;* while there, he established close relationships with leading authors of the time.

MARY ADAMS (seventeenth century), British writer, about whom little is known. According to *Early Modern Poets: An Anthology* (2001), she was a working-class prophetess, perhaps connected with a Baptist minister called Richard Adams, who published a two-page pamphlet in 1676 called *A Warning to the Inhabitants of England and London in Particular.*

PATIENCE AGBABI (1965–), British poet and performer, often explores the combination of spoken-word poetry with traditional poetic forms. Her first collection, *R.A.W.,* was awarded the 1997 Excelle Literary Award. From 1999 to 2000 Agbabi held the post of "in-house poet" at Flamin' Eight, a tattoo and piercing studio located in her native London.

A. ALVAREZ (1929–), British poet, is well known for both his creative and critical work, especially *The Savage God: A Study of Suicide*. Born in London, Alvarez served as poetry editor and critic for the *Observer* from 1955 to 1956. In 1961 he was awarded the Vachel Lindsay Prize for Poetry.

MONIZA ALVI (1954–), Pakistani-British poet, moved from Lahore to London when only a few months old. She has taught at both the Scott Lidgett School and the Aylwin School in London, earning her M.A. in education from the London University Institute of Education in 1985. In 2002 she received the Cholmondeley Award.

TALVIKKI ANSEL (1962–), American poet, attended Indiana University for her M.F.A. and Stanford University as a Wallace Stegner fellow. Her first collection, *My Shining Archipelago,* one sequence of which imagines Shakespeare's Caliban relocated to Elizabethan London, was selected for the 1996 Yale Younger Poets Award. Her second book of poems, *Jetty,* was published in 2003.

MATTHEW ARNOLD (1822–1888), British poet, is representative of Victorian aesthetic taste and style. In 1847 he moved to London to work as Lord Lansdowne's private secretary; during this time, he wrote and published his first two volumes of poetry. Over the course of his life, he also became well known for his literary and social criticism, including *Culture and Anarchy.*

JOHN BANCKS (1709–1751), British poet, was a weaver's apprentice who lived in London, where he also entered the service of a bookseller and bookbinder. His works include two books of poems, including a "Life of Christ" and an account of Oliver Cromwell.

TED BERRIGAN (1934–1983), American poet, is considered a member of the second generation of the New York School of Poets. In 1964 he privately published *The Sonnets,* which has since become the centerpiece of his oeuvre. An expansive personality and well-loved teacher, Berrigan taught at universities in both the United States and England.

WILLIAM BLAKE (1757–1827), British poet, engraver, and painter, spent the majority of his life in London. Blake wrote and illustrated such works as *Songs of Innocence and Experience, The Book of Thel,* and *The Marriage of Heaven and Hell.* He held radical political and religious beliefs for his time and heavily influenced British Romanticism.

EAVAN BOLAND (1944–), Irish poet, grew up in Dublin, London, and New York City. She established herself as a female Irish poet, placing particular emphasis on the domestic and on viewing women as more than national or poetic symbols. Her many awards include a Lannan Foundation Award in Poetry and the John Frederick Nims Memorial Prize.

JORGE LUIS BORGES (1899–1986), Argentine poet, author, and translator, is most famous for his fantastical short stories. Themes of time, questions of identity, and images of labyrinths abound in his work. Internationally revered, he was the recipient of such diverse honors as the Prix Formentor, the Miguel de Cervantes Award, the French Legion of Honor, and the Jerusalem Prize.

ROBERT BRIDGES (1844–1930), British poet, studied at Corpus Christi College, Oxford, before earning his M.B. in 1874 at St. Bartholomew's Hospital in London. He worked as a physician until 1882, after which he dedicated himself entirely to writing. Bridges often experimented with syllabic-based meter; later readers consider *The Testament of Beauty* to be his most enduring work. For a time he was poet laureate of England.

JOSEPH BRODSKY (1940–1996), Russian poet, won the Nobel Prize for Literature and once served as poet laureate for the United States. Brodsky was exiled from the Soviet Union in 1972; before finally settling in the United States, he lived briefly in both Vienna and London. He is considered to be a major international poet of the twentieth century.

ELIZABETH BARRETT BROWNING (1806–1861), British poet, was married to Robert Browning. She was greatly respected by her contemporaries for such works as *Sonnets from the Portuguese,* a collection of intense love poems. She lived in London before emigrating to Florence, and is still regarded as an influential Victorian writer.

ROBERT BROWNING (1812–1889), British poet, known for his dramatic monologues, was married to Elizabeth Barrett Browning. He wrote extensively—both poetry and plays—before his contemporary readers fully recognized his talents in the 1860s with such publications as *Dramatis Personae* and *The Ring and the Book.* Browning lived in London for the majority of his life.

RACHAEL CASTELETE (1884?–1966), Greek poet, was the daughter of a notable collector and performer of Judezmo folk songs. She moved to London in 1913. She is the author of a chapbook of poems, in which the Judezmo original of "When I Came to London" appears.

AMARJIT CHANDAN (1946–), Punjabi poet, was born in Kenya and raised in India, where he matriculated at the Panjab University; in 1980 he moved to London. Chandan has written eight collections of Punjabi poetry and served as editor of two

British Punjabi anthologies. In 2002 he received the Shiromani Punjabi Bideshi Sahitkar Award.

AMY CLAMPITT (1920–1994), American poet, born in Iowa, moved to New York City after graduating from college; her first trip to London was in 1949. Originally interested in writing novels, Clampitt did not receive major recognition for her poems until the publication of *The Kingfisher* when she was sixty-three. Her poems are often praised for their complex syntax, vocabulary, and use of allusion.

ARTHUR HUGH CLOUGH (1819–1861), British poet during the Victorian era. In 1848, as a result of his growing religious doubts, he resigned from Oxford University; the following year, he accepted the position of head of school for University Hall, London. Works such as *Dipsychus* and *Amours de Voyage* are notable for their use of irony and skepticism.

JEAN COCTEAU (1889–1963), French poet, novelist, dramatist, painter, and filmmaker, insisted that all of his work (regardless of medium) was poetry. He is well known for *Les enfants terribles, Le sang d'un poète,* and his 1946 film *La belle et la bête.* In 1960 Cocteau completed a mural of the crucifixion for Notre-Dame de France in London.

MARY COLERIDGE (1861–1907), British poet, novelist, and essayist, was born in London. During her lifetime she enjoyed popular success with novels such as *The King with Two Faces;* however, her poems have since garnered recognition. In addition to writing, Coleridge taught at the Working Women's College in London from 1895 until her death.

MERLE COLLINS (1950–), Grenadian poet, novelist, and short fiction writer, emigrated to Britain in the 1980s. Once in London, Collins taught at the University of North London and earned her doctorate in government from the University of London, School of Economics and Political Science. Her poems often incorporate Caribbean dialect and culture.

STEPHEN CUSHMAN (1956–), American poet, is the author of three collections of poetry, most recently *Heart Island,* as well as two critical works. Cushman is Robert C. Taylor Professor of English Literature at the University of Virginia; he has frequently taught in the university's Culture of London summer program.

DAVID DABYDEEN (1955–), Guyanese poet, also writes fiction and nonfiction. In 1969 he moved to England, eventually earning his doctorate from University College London. His many awards include the Quiller-Couch Prize and the Commonwealth Poetry Prize; he has published three collections of poetry and four novels.

FRED D'AGUIAR (1960–), British poet, novelist, and dramatist. His first novel, *The Longest Memory,* received the David Higham First Novel Award and the 1995 Whitbread Award. After graduating from the University of Kent, D'Aguiar was writer-in-residence for the London borough of Lewisham. He currently serves as codirector of the M.F.A. program in creative writing at Virginia Tech.

JOHN DAVIDSON (1857–1909), Scottish poet, playwright, and novelist, moved to London in 1890 in hopes of enhancing his literary career. In the mid-1890s he achieved recognition for *Fleet Street Eclogues* and *Ballads and Songs,* both collections of poetry; however, he was unable to maintain this level of success, and he eventually committed suicide in 1909.

WALTER DE LA MARE (1873–1956), British poet and novelist. From 1890 to 1908 he worked for the Anglo-American Oil Company in London, gradually devoting more and more time to his writing. *Songs of Childhood,* a collection of poetry, established de la Mare as a leading writer of children's literature.

MICHAEL DONAGHY (1954–2004), American poet and musician, graduated from Fordham University in 1976 and earned his master's degree from the University of Chicago. In 1985 he moved to London, residing there until his death. *Shibboleth,* published in 1988, won the Whitbread Award and the Geoffrey Faber Award.

JOHN DRYDEN (1631–1700), British poet, dramatist, translator, and influential prose stylist. His epic poem *Annus Mirabilis* commemorates the Great Fire of London and contributed to Dryden's receiving the poet laureateship in 1668. The poems *Absalom and Achitophel, Mac Flecknoe,* and later his translations of Virgil, earned Dryden the esteem of his contemporaries and a central role in seventeenth-century English literature.

CAROL ANN DUFFY (1955–), Scottish poet and playwright, is often noted for her use of dramatic monologue to feature otherwise marginalized voices. Duffy moved to London in the early 1980s, where, beginning in 1983, she worked as poetry editor for *Ambit.* Her numerous awards include a T. S. Eliot Prize for *Rapture,* her most recent poetry collection.

PAUL LAURENCE DUNBAR (1872–1906), American poet and novelist, was one of the first nationally recognized black writers in the United States; in 1897 he gave a series of readings in England. Although works such as *Majors and Minors* exhibit Dunbar's ability to write in both standard English and dialect, his popularity during his lifetime was largely built on his use of dialect alone.

T. S. ELIOT (1888–1965), American-British poet and playwright, moved to London in 1914 and became a naturalized British subject in 1927. From 1917 to 1925 Eliot worked as a clerk at Lloyd's Bank in London. *The Waste Land* and *Four Quartets* are considered two of the finest works of the modernist era, and his many prizes include an Order of Merit and the 1948 Nobel Prize in Literature.

CARRIE ETTER (1969–), American poet, born in Normal, Illinois, moved to England in 2001, where she is a lecturer in creative writing at Bath Spa University. Her poems have appeared in journals in both the United States and the United Kingdom, including the *New Republic* and the *Times Literary Supplement*. Etter holds an M.F.A. and Ph.D. from the University of California at Irvine.

BERNARDINE EVARISTO (1959–), British poet and novelist. *Lara,* her first novel in verse, explores the ancestry and personal difficulties of a young, interracial woman in 1960s London; the work received the EMMA Best Novel Award in 1999. That same year Evaristo served as poet-in-residence at the Museum of London. Her most recent work is a novel in verse entitled *Soul Tourists.*

STEVE GEHRKE (1971–), American poet, earned his M.F.A. at the University of Texas at Austin as a James Michener Fellow. He is the author of three collections of poetry, most recently *Michelangelo's Seizure,* which won the National Poetry Series Award and was published in 2007. His other awards include the Philip Levine Prize, a Pushcart Prize, and a grant from the National Endowment for the Arts. Gehrke teaches at Seton Hall University in New Jersey.

LAVINIA GREENLAW (1962–), British poet and novelist, graduated from the London College of Printing and earned her master's degree from the University of London. Greenlaw has worked as an editor for London publishers and as writer-in-residence for London's Science Museum. Her most recent collection of poems, *Minsk,* was short-listed for both the T. S. Eliot Prize and the Whitbread Award.

EAMON GRENNAN (1941–), Irish poet. His first collection of poems, *Wildly for Days,* appeared in 1983, and he has published regularly since then. In 1997 his translation of Giacomo Leopardi earned him a PEN Award for Poetry Translation. Grennan teaches at Vassar College in Poughkeepsie, New York.

H. D. (1886–1961), American poet, also known as Hilda Doolittle, was linked with both the imagist and modernist movements. In 1911 H. D. traveled to Europe, reconnecting with Ezra Pound in London; at this time she met both Ford Maddox Ford and Richard Aldington. Though primarily known for her imagistic verse, such as "Oread," H. D. also published plays, translations, and novels. Her third major novel, *Bid Me to Live,* depicts life in 1920s London.

JAMES HARPUR (1956–), poet of Irish-British descent, attended Cambridge University and has published three collections of poetry, most recently *Oracle Bones.* His honors include a 1985 Eric Gregory Award and a 2001 Year of the Artist Award.

LEE HARWOOD (1939–), British poet, born in Leicester, obtained his B.A. from Queen Mary College, London, in 1961. He won the Alice Hunt Bartlett Prize in 1976 and released his *Collected Poems* in 2004. Harwood has been associated with the New York School poets and the Dadaists, and has translated the poems of Tristan Tzara.

ROBERT HAYDEN (1913–1980), American poet, born in Detroit, Michigan. After earning his B.A., Hayden worked for the Federal

Writers' Project, conducting research on African American history and culture in the United States; his poems frequently utilize historical facts or figures. In 1966 his collection *A Ballad of Remembrance* received the grand prize at the First World Festival of Negro Arts.

SEAMUS HEANEY (1939–), Irish poet and translator, was born in Northern Ireland. His poetry often fuses Irish mythology with contemporary concerns, Irish history with daily life. His many honors include the 1995 Nobel Prize for Literature, a Cholmondeley Award, and two Whitbread Awards—one in recognition of his modern translation of *Beowulf.* Over the course of his career, Heaney has given many readings in London.

ROBERT HERRICK (1591–1674), British poet, was born in London. Initially apprenticed to a goldsmith, Herrick eventually attended Cambridge University, where in 1623 he was ordained a cleric. He is best known for his lyric poems, often addressed to women, such as "Upon Julia's Clothes" and "To the Virgins, to Make Much of Time."

MAX HERSHMAN (1891–?), Yiddish poet, was born in Kiev in the Ukraine. Hershman settled in London in 1912.

MIROSLAV HOLUB (1923–1998), Czech poet and immunologist, received his M.D. from Charles University School of Medicine in 1953. During his life, Holub held such varied positions as clinical pathologist, scientific worker, and writer-in-residence, and his poetry often incorporates scientific knowledge. In 1975 he read at the Cambridge Poetry Festival in England.

MICHAEL HOROVITZ (1935–), poet, born in Germany, moved to England in 1937. He founded *New Departures* magazine in 1959, also serving as editor and publisher; that same year, he began his "Live New Departures" shows, which emphasize the experiential aspects of poetry. His most recent work is *A New Waste Land: Timeship Earth at Nillennium*.

TED HUGHES (1930–1998), British poet, married to Sylvia Plath. Hughes's poetry frequently employs imagery from the natural world, emphasizing its violence while evoking archetypal figures, as in *The Hawk in the Rain* and *Crow*. He was a founding editor of the series Modern Poetry in Translation and served as Britain's poet laureate from 1984 until his death.

RANDALL JARRELL (1914–1965), American poet. In 1942 he joined the U.S. Army Air Force and published his first collection, *Blood for a Stranger*. A leading voice in twentieth-century criticism, Jarrell demanded that readers recognize the talents of then-neglected poets such as Walt Whitman and Robert Frost. He is well known for his war-influenced poems and for his late-career dramatic monologues.

LINTON KWESI JOHNSON (1952–), Jamaican poet and musician, emigrated to England in 1963. He graduated from Goldsmith's College at the University of London and was a founding member of the Race Today Collective. Johnson is a leading dub poet and has recorded his poetry to reggae music, for example, his album *Dread, Beat, and Blood*. The subject of his poem "New Craas Massakah," the New Cross Fire, also called the Deptford Fire, was a racially motivated arson attack at a birthday party in 1981.

LIONEL JOHNSON (1867–1902), British poet and critic, moved to London in 1890. He wrote essays for the *National Observer* and published *The Art of Thomas Hardy;* he also belonged to the Rhymers' Club. In 1902 he died from a skull fracture. Ezra Pound later claimed it was caused by falling off a barstool, a detail that W. B. Yeats incorporated into the poem "In Memory of Major Robert Gregory."

NISHIWAKI JUNZABURŌ (1894–1982), Japanese poet and critic, studied Old and Middle English at Oxford University. While in London, Junzaburō published *Spectrum,* a collection of poems written entirely in English. He also wrote poetry in Japanese and translated many famous English writers, including William Shakespeare and T. S. Eliot.

RUDYARD KIPLING (1865–1936), British novelist, short-story writer, and poet, was born in India. He moved to England in 1871, later returning to India to work as a journalist; at the same time he published poetry and fiction, including the story "The Man Who Would Be King." Kipling also established himself in the genre of children's literature, creating such classics as *The Jungle Book.* In "London Stone," he grieves for his son, lost in battle in World War I. Kipling is buried in Westminster Abbey in London.

VALERY LARBAUD (1881–1957), French novelist and critic, was celebrated for his creation of A. O. Barnabooth, a fictional South American millionaire and poet in *Poèmes par un riche amateur.* Larbaud was also an excellent translator, assisting in the translation of Joyce's *Ulysses* into French. In 1914 he contributed a series of articles to London's *New Weekly.*

PHILIP LARKIN (1922–1985), British poet and novelist, lived his entire life in England. From 1943 until his death, Larkin worked as a librarian while pursuing his own writing; he also spent ten years as a jazz critic for London's *Daily Telegraph.* He is well loved and respected for such collections as *The Whitsun Weddings* and *High Windows.*

D. H. LAWRENCE (1885–1930), British poet, short-story writer, and novelist, is most famous for his novels, such as *Lady Chatterley's Lover.* In 1908 Lawrence moved to London for a teaching position;

after 1911 writing became his primary occupation. Owing to his sensual and often explicit prose, Lawrence saw many of his works, including *The Rainbow,* banned or censored during his lifetime.

HERBERT LOMAS (1924–), British poet and translator. In 1950 he began his teaching career, holding positions in Greece and Finland before becoming a lecturer at the West London Institute of Higher Education. His collection *Letters in the Dark* is based on his visits to Southwark Cathedral in London, and his translations of contemporary Finnish poetry and prose have been widely lauded.

ROBERT LOWELL (1917–1977), American poet, began writing in traditional meter but soon became a leader of the so-called confessional poets. His 1959 collection *Life Studies* relied heavily on autobiography and earned Lowell a National Book Award. During the 1970s Lowell lived in England, lecturing at various universities and frequenting London.

LOUIS MACNEICE (1907–1963), British poet and playwright, born in Belfast. After graduating from Oxford University, MacNeice taught for four years at the Bedford College for Women in London. Although respected for his poetry, MacNeice is better known for his radio and television plays, such as *The Dark Tower,* many of which were produced on the BBC.

CHARLOTTE MEW (1869–1928), British poet and short-story writer, was born and raised in London. Although Mew began publishing stories in 1894, it was her poetry that caught the attention of her contemporaries, including Thomas Hardy and Virginia Woolf; she published her first collection, *The Farmer's Bride,* in 1916. In her poems she favored the dramatic monologue, as in "Madeleine in Church" and "The Fête." After a lifetime of struggling with depression, she died by her own hand.

ADRIAN MITCHELL (1932–), British poet, playwright, and fiction writer, also worked as a journalist for various London newspapers. His work, often political, promotes pacifism, and his poems combine an agile imagination with direct speech; he has also adapted classic children's stories into plays, such as *The Snow Queen*. From 1982 to 1983 he served as resident writer for London's Unicorn Theatre for Children.

EUGENIO MONTALE (1896–1981), Italian poet and translator, received an honorary degree from Cambridge University and was awarded the Nobel Prize for Literature. Montale's lyric poems often rely on symbols or on absent beloveds to explore emotion, and his work helped to modernize Italian poetry. He also translated numerous English writers into Italian, including William Shakespeare and T. S. Eliot.

ANDREW MOTION (1952–), British poet, worked as poetry editor for London's *Poetry Review* from 1981 to 1983. His first collection of poems, *The Pleasure Steamers,* demonstrated his gift for expressing and exploring both loss and anguish, as well as his imaginative use of past figures or events to explore contemporary or personal feelings. Motion has earned numerous awards and currently serves as Britain's poet laureate.

CAROL MUSKE-DUKES (1945–), American poet and novelist, founded and codirects the doctoral program in creative writing and literature at the University of Southern California. Her poems are contemplative and well crafted, often using personal experience as a springboard into meditation, as in her most recent collection, *Sparrow.* Muske-Dukes's many honors include the Alice Fay Di Castagnola Award and several Pushcart Prizes.

EILÉAN NÍ CHUILLEANÁIN (1942–), Irish poet, earned degrees at University College, Cork, and Oxford University. Her first collection of poems, *Acts and Monuments,* won the Patrick Kavanagh Award for Poetry, and she cofounded the Irish literary magazine *Cyphers.* Her poems are distinctive in their imaginative use of mythology and in their oblique and often hidden use of personal or contemporary experience.

BEN OKRI (1959–), Nigerian novelist and poet, spent part of his early childhood in south London and moved to London permanently in 1978. His novels are associated with magical realism, and Okri often uses dreamlike or mystical imagery to examine political instability and the effects of civil war. His novel *The Famished Road* was awarded the 1991 Booker Prize.

WILFRED OWEN (1893–1918), British poet, enlisted in the army in 1915 and trained in London, making frequent visits to Harold Monro's Poetry Bookshop; Owen was killed in battle in 1918. His poems, such as "Dulce et Decorum Est," explore the complicated mix of feelings evoked by and experienced during war, especially anger, melancholy, and compassion. His poems also make wonderful use of both assonance and partial rhyme.

ERIC PANKEY (1959–), American poet, earned his M.F.A. at the University of Iowa and teaches at George Mason University. His first collection of poems, *For the New Year,* received the 1984 Walt Whitman Award; more recently, *Cenotaph* was selected for the Library of Virginia's Poetry Award.

COVENTRY PATMORE (1823–1896), British poet and essayist. From 1846 to 1865 he worked as a librarian at the British Museum in London, reading and writing poetry in his spare time. *The Unknown Eros and Other Odes* explores both spiritual love and married love, employs nontraditional lineation, and is generally considered to contain his finest poems.

SYLVIA PLATH (1932–1963), American poet, was married for a time to Ted Hughes. Plath published one book of poems during her lifetime; however, she is best remembered for her intensely emotional and often autobiographical poems in *Ariel,* a posthumous publication. She committed suicide in London at the peak of her writing prowess.

KATHLEEN RAINE (1908–2003), British poet and critic, earned a master's degree from Cambridge University and later lectured at Morley College, London. She produced an extensive body of work, often noted for its mystical qualities as well for its focus on the natural world, and became a leading scholar of both William Blake and W. B. Yeats.

ARTHUR RIMBAUD (1854–1891), French poet, envisioned the poet as a medium through which we encounter the eternal or otherworldly. His poems in *Illuminations,* including prose poems and free verse poems, experiment wildly with punctuation, vocabulary, and form. He traveled to London in 1872 with his then lover and fellow poet Paul Verlaine.

ANTHONY RUDOLF (1942–), British poet, translator, and editor, cofounded Menard Press, which specializes in English translations and is located in London. *Mandorla* is his most recent collection of poems. He is also well known for his translations of Yves Bonnefoy's poetry and was appointed Chevalier de l'Ordre des Arts et des Lettres in 2004.

ANDREW SALKEY (1928–1995), poet of Caribbean descent, was born in Panama and raised in Jamaica. Salkey worked for the BBC from 1952 to 1956, conducting interviews, writing scripts, and editing programs; he graduated from the University of London in 1955. In addition to writing poetry, Salkey also wrote novels, short stories, and children's literature.

JAROSLAV SEIFERT (1901–1986), Czech poet, received the Nobel Prize for Literature in 1984. In addition to lyrical love poetry, Seifert also wrote political poems opposing communism; his devotion to his homeland as well as his use of direct language earned him the devotion of his countrymen. *An Umbrella from Piccadilly* was one of the first of his collections to be translated into English.

RAVI SHANKAR (1975–), Indian-American poet, is the founding editor of the international online journal of the arts *Drunken Boat*. He is poet-in-residence at Central Connecticut State University and the author of a book of poems, *Instrumentality*. Shankar, a finalist for the 2005 Connecticut Book Awards, has appeared as a commentator on National Public Radio; published work in the *Paris Review, McSweeney's,* and *Poets & Writers;* and is currently editing an anthology of contemporary Asian and Arab poetry.

IAIN SINCLAIR (1943–), British poet, novelist, and filmmaker, studied at both Trinity College, Dublin, and what is now the London Film School. Whatever the medium, Sinclair's primary fascination has always been London, and works such as *Lud Heat* and *White Chappell: Scarlet Tracings* center on and incorporate London's history. His *London: City of Disappearances* is an exciting "autobiography" of this shape-shifting city.

DAME EDITH SITWELL (1887–1964), British poet, spent much of her life in England and died in London. Throughout her career, Sitwell emphasized and experimented with the musicality and rhythms of poetry, as in *Façade;* her later collections also employ spiritual symbolism. In 1954 she was the first poet to be named Dame of the British Empire.

LYTTON SMITH (1982–), British poet, was born in Galleywood, England, lived in London for several years, and currently resides in New York City, where he is studying Anglo-Saxon literature. He is author of the chapbook *Monster Theory* and a graduate of Columbia University's M.F.A. program.

PRISCILLA SNEFF (1956–), American poet, teaches creative writing at Tufts University. She has published poems in numerous literary journals, including the *Yale Review, Ploughshares,* and the *Kenyon Review,* and her first collection, *O Woolly City,* was published in 2007. Her awards include the 2004 Kenyon Review Poetry Prize and a fellowship from the National Endowment for the Arts.

GERTRUDE STEIN (1874–1946), American poet, left Johns Hopkins Medical School to move to London, then Paris. In Paris, Stein established a famous salon where she promoted the work of Pablo Picasso and Ernest Hemingway, among others. Stein's highly experimental writing, including *Tender Buttons,* relies on images, repetition, and fragmentation as opposed to conventional narrative or poetic techniques.

AVRAM NOCHUM STENCL (1897–1983), Yiddish poet, was born in Poland and arrived in London in November 1936. He served as editor of *Loshen und Leben* (Language and Life), a monthly periodical. Stencl lived in and often wrote about London's East End.

GRETA STODDART (1966–), British poet, was born in Henley-on-Thames and now lives in London. Her first collection, *At Home in the Dark,* received the 2002 Geoffrey Faber Memorial Prize. Stoddart serves as writer-in-residence at the University of Exeter and also works as a poetry tutor.

DYLAN THOMAS (1914–1953), Welsh poet. In the mid-1930s Thomas moved to London, where he wrote scripts and provided radio commentary on poetry for the BBC. His poems are highly musical and emotional, often inventing rhythms and creating a complex syntax; his later poems frequently employ religious symbolism. His poem "A Refusal to Mourn the Death, by Fire, of a Child in London" was written after a German V-2 rocket killed a child in London during World War II.

JON THOMPSON (1959–   ), American poet, was born in Ohio and teaches at North Carolina State University. Thompson did a B.A. and M.A. at University College, Dublin, and a Ph.D. in English and American Literature at Louisiana State University. His first collection, *The Book of the Floating World,* was published in 2004 and will appear in a new edition in 2007. Thompson is also the founding editor of *Free Verse: A Journal of Contemporary Poetry and Poetics* and Free Verse Editions. "The Sky Comes Down to Earth" is from a new collection, *Strange Country.*

GEORGE TURBERVILLE (C. 1540–C. 1610), British poet and translator, studied law in London and served as secretary to the first English ambassador to Russia. With his book *Epitaphes, Epigrams, Songs and Sonets,* Turberville became one of the first English writers to publish verses addressed to his lady, thereby helping to establish a poetic tradition.

PAUL VERLAINE (1844–1896), French poet, was associated with the decadent movement as well as with the later symbolists. His troubled relationship with the poet Arthur Rimbaud resulted in Verlaine's imprisonment, during which time his *Romances sans paroles* was published. After serving a two-year sentence, Verlaine lived and taught briefly in London before returning to his native France.

DEREK WALCOTT (1930–   ), West Indian poet and playwright, writes primarily in English and consistently explores the inter-section of races and cultures, specifically the effects of British co-lonialism on the Caribbean. He is perhaps most famous for his epic poem *Omeros,* which draws upon Homer's *Iliad* and *Odyssey* while employing Dante's terza rima. In 1992 he received the Nobel Prize for Literature.

OSCAR WILDE (1854–1900), Irish poet, playwright, novelist, and critic, was one of the leading figures of late nineteenth-century aestheticism. After graduating from Oxford University, Wilde moved to London where, from 1887 to 1889, he edited *Woman's World;* in 1895 he was sentenced to two years in prison for homosexual acts. He is best remembered for his novel *The Picture of Dorian Gray,* and his satirical plays *Lady Windermere's Fan* and *The Importance of Being Earnest.*

WILLIAM WORDSWORTH (1770–1850), British poet and critic. With Samuel Taylor Coleridge, Wordsworth compiled the poems of *Lyrical Ballads;* this publication is considered the beginning of British Romanticism. Wordsworth traveled to France and Germany and lived for a short period in London, ultimately settling in the Lake District.

CHARLES WRIGHT (1935–), American poet, translator, and essayist, was born in Pickwick Dam, Tennessee. Wright won the 1998 Pulitzer Prize for his collection *Black Zodiac.* His many honors include the National Book Award, an Ingram Merrill Fellowship, and the Lenore Marshall poetry prize. He teaches at the University of Virginia.

YANG LIAN (1955–), Chinese–New Zealand poet, born in Switzerland and educated in Beijing. After the Tiananmen Square massacre in 1989, Yang participated in protests in New Zealand; as a result, his Chinese citizenship was revoked and he has lived in London since the early 1990s. In 1999 he received the Flaiano International Prize for Poetry.

PETER YATES (1909–1976), American poet and music critic, published *A Smaller Poem Book* in 1946. Through works such as *An Amateur at the Keyboard* and events such as his so-called Evenings on the Roof, Yates promoted a less professionalized and more direct approach to contemporary music.

DAVID YOUNG (1936–), American poet and translator, has published numerous collections of poetry, most recently *Black Lab*. Since 1986 he has been the Longman Professor of English at Oberlin College, and he has edited *Field* magazine since 1969. His many honors include the 1968 U.S. Award at the International Poetry Forum and a National Endowment for the Humanities fellowship in England.

Copyright Acknowledgments

Grateful acknowledgment is made to reprint the following copyrighted works. Every attempt has been made to trace copyright holders. The editor and the publisher would be interested in hearing from anyone not here acknowledged.

Dannie Abse: "Soho: Saturday Night." From *New and Collected Poems* by Dannie Abse, published by Hutchinson. Reprinted by permission of The Random House Group Ltd.

J. R. Ackerley: "The Conjurer on Hammersmith Bridge." From *Micheldever and Other Poems* by J. R. Ackerley, published by Ian McKelvie. Copyright © 1973 by J. R. Ackerley. Reprinted by permission of David Higham Associates Limited.

Patience Agbabi: "The London Eye." From *Earth Has Not Any Thing To Shew More Fair,* edited by Peter Oswald and Alice Oswald and Robert Woof (Shakespeare's Globe & The Wordsworth Trust, 2002) and subsequently produced as a Poem on the Underground Poster (Cassell, 2003), reprinted in two *Poems on the Underground* anthologies (Cassell, 2004, 2006). Copyright © Patience Agbabi. Reprinted by permission of the author.

A. Alvarez: "Mourning and Melancholia." From *Autumn to Autumn and Selected Poems, 1953–76* by A. Alvarez, published by Macmillan. Copyright © 1978 by A. Alvarez. Reprinted by permission of Gillon Aitken Associates.

Moniza Alvi: "The Double City." From *Carrying My Wife* by Moniza Alvi, published by Bloodaxe Books, 2000. Reprinted by permission of Bloodaxe Books.

Index